Prestel Museum Guide
Bröhan-Museum

BRÖHAN-MUSEUM
Berlin

Art Nouveau
Art Deco
Functionalism

Prestel
Munich · Berlin · London · New York

Foreword

The Bröhan-Museum in Charlottenburg, Berlin
From private collection to state museum

'What started out as a private museum in a large middle-class villa in Dahlem (Berlin) is now part of the museum complex at Charlottenburg Palace. That is in a nutshell the story of my art collection over its 25-year history,' wrote the museum's founder and first director Karl H. Bröhan in a foreword to our publication celebrating its 27th anniversary in 1998.

The Bröhan-Museum passed into the care of the federal state of Berlin in 1994, becoming the state museum for Art Nouveau, Art Deco and Functionalism and covering the period 1889 to 1939. Its collection includes fully-furnished rooms presenting in context items of international Art Nouveau and Art Deco such as furniture, carpets, lighting, silver and metal pieces, glass, porcelain and pottery. Along with the field of applied art, the corpus of Berlin Secession paintings and graphic art is a major constituent of the collection in the museum.

Karl H. Bröhan (6 July 1921–2 January 2000) came originally from Hamburg, but celebrated his 60th birthday by donating his extensive collection of art objects to his adopted home Berlin. Following work on converting the new premises at Charlottenburger Schloßstrasse 1a under the guidance of architect Winnetou Kampmann, the present home of the museum was opened in 1983, though at that date only the ground floor was available. The neo-classical building was previously an infantry barracks, forming part of the palace ensemble. The official opening took place on 14th October, with the Berlin mayor of the time, Richard von Weizsäcker (later the federal president), performing the honours.

Bröhan initially established a reputation as a collector of 18th-century Berlin porcelain, but he then focused on a new period of interest, Art Nouveau, concentrating particularly on porcelain from the major European manufactories. Art Nouveau porcelain is uncommonly diverse. It embraces a wide variety of makers, including famous names ranging from Royal Copenhagen and Bing & Grøndahl (Denmark), KPM, Meissen and Nymphenburg (Germany), Sèvres (France), Rozenburg (Holland), Rörstrand (Sweden) to Bohemian/Czech porcelain. All the leading designers and manufacturers are represented in the museum, and their products are on show in the permanent collection, if at times only selectively due to problems of space.

The core collection of the museum also includes extensive holdings of modernist glassware. A particular strength is the large collection of Bohemian lustre ware by Loetz Witwe, a fascinating spectrum of this special type of Art Nouveau glassware. Unique pieces by the great name of Nancy glassware, Emile Gallé, indicate the quality of the exhibits.

The collection of silverware and other metal pieces has also been steadily expanded, and the Bröhan-Museum now has one of the most extensive arrays of luxury and domestic utensils from the period 1889–1939. The great designers and manufacturing businesses such as Georg Jensen, Christopher Dresser, Archibald Knox, Jan Eisenlöffel, Jean Puiforcat, Friedrich Adler and Joseph Maria Olbrich are all represented with excellent works.

Alongside his role as founding director, Karl Bröhan remained active as the museum's collector-patron. The new premises soon reached full capacity, but through good fortune and thanks to the support of the Berlin Senate the third floor of the building was made available to the museum in 1990. Conversion work to make the large, light-filled space suitable for museum purposes, particularly for special presentations with a gallery of showcases all around, was undertaken by Hilde Weström. Two side rooms are devoted to the important, pioneering artists of modernism, Henry van de Velde and Josef Hoffmann, who are both represented with outstanding, select works.

Prof. Karl-H. Bröhan and Dr. Margrit Bröhan, 1998

Besides applied art, the collection and scholarly study of the oeuvres of painters of the Berlin Secession is a prime concern of the Bröhan-Museum. Hans Baluschek, Karl Hagemeister, Walter Leistikow and Willy Jaeckel are well represented in an extensive selection of works. Solo exhibitions with accompanying publications were organised for them, this being a special interest of Margrit Bröhan, who made a particular study of these artists.

In 1998, a further floor of the building was acquired for use as a picture gallery, which opened in December that year with a large and very successful retrospective of the work of Karl Hagemeister.

In its first fifteen years in Charlottenburg, the Bröhan-Museum proved itself to be not just a successful museum with a taste for expansion. Items in its collection were also much in demand for major international exhibitions, and the museum organised special exhibitions inhouse from its own collections. Along with the general museum activities, the museum put in hand a programme of academic publications about the collection. Karl Bröhan himself was naturally passionately interested in the items in the collection, but was concerned that they should also get their scholarly due as well, and therefore initiated the publication of a series of catalogues about the collection. The seven solid volumes in the series now provide an extraordinarily good scholarly and photographic record of the exhibits. They have proved their worth internationally, some having been sold out, and have been reissued in revised, expanded editions. Karl Bröhan set high standards with these publications.

In both its original aim and its collecting policy, the Bröhan is a museum about a particular period, a specialist museum that gave equal status to all forms of art within that period. This was a particular feature of international styles around 1900, moving many artists of that generation to give up painting in favour of the applied arts. Initially, Karl Bröhan's interest focused on furniture pieces and objets d'art by French Art Nouveau and Art Deco designers such as Hector Guimard, Eugène Gaillard, Emile Gallé and Jacques-Emile Ruhlmann, finding in them the ultimate artistic sophistication that gave him most pleasure. It was not until later that the German reform movement with artists such as Peter Behrens and Richard Riemerschmid were included in the collecting policy. Not surprisingly, one of the major attractions of the museum is its origin as a private collection, reflecting the preferences and knowledge of a collector and conveying his passion for the objects in visible form.

The death of Karl Bröhan in 2000 inevitably involved the museum in a degree of re-orientation. The idea of going for

Foreword

ensemble effects was expanded and opened up. This is when we came up with the idea of 'country profiles' showing art around 1900 in international comparison. Unlike pure art museums, we were in the happy position of being able to show all aspects of the new style and could therefore document the integral nature of the reform movement in artistic terms.

A start was made in 2000 with a large special exhibition about French Art Nouveau, in collaboration with Mathildenhöhe in Darmstadt. Subsequently we put on exhibitions conceived and organised inhouse, such as 'Now the Light Comes from the North'—Art Nouveau in Finland (2002/2003)—a joint venture with leading Finnish museums—and most recently 'Beauty for Everyone' (2005/2006), an exhibition about Swedish Art Nouveau.

In each case, the underlying concept was to exhibit a mixture of paintings by leading artists of the country concerned plus pieces of applied art. Almost all these major exhibitions, which covered new artistic terrain, were supported by the Stiftung Deutsche Klassenlotterie and the Hauptstadtkulturfonds, and we should like to put our gratitude to them on record here.

The commitment that informed the life and work of Karl H. Bröhan was continued by Margrit Bröhan (director, 2000–2003), though on a different basis. It was due to her initiative that a support body (Friends of the Bröhan-Museum), was set up in 2004, turning for the first time to the public and bringing in private individuals who would be willing to provide assistance to the museum. The present publication was made possible thanks to the generous support of the Friends.

The Bröhan-Museum is now in demand for international museum co-operations , often in collaboration with representatives of politics and the diplomatic service. Links to academic research and teaching have been consolidated with the granting and acceptance of teaching commissions at the *Freie Universität* in Berlin. Our thematic special exhibitions have featured academic symposia organised jointly with the *Freie Universität*, when international experts from museums and universities have explored various aspects of art around 1900. Our institution is thus an important cultural factor in Berlin that has also demonstrated its relevance in an international context.

Looking back to the idyllic days when the Bröhan collection was a private museum housed in a villa in Max Eyth Strasse in Dahlem, we can see that the institution has come a long way, developing unusually but consistently. Many of our visitors were familiar with the collection from the very beginning and lament the passing of that very personal and intimate atmosphere. Yet despite the great variety of our activities, the care and presentation of its own extensive and exclusive collection in the Bröhan-Museum today—Berlin's own museum for Art Nouveau, Art Deco and Functionalism from 1889 to 1939—still claim first priority. The legacy of the past imposes a duty for the future.

Dr. Ingeborg Becker
Director, Bröhan-Museum

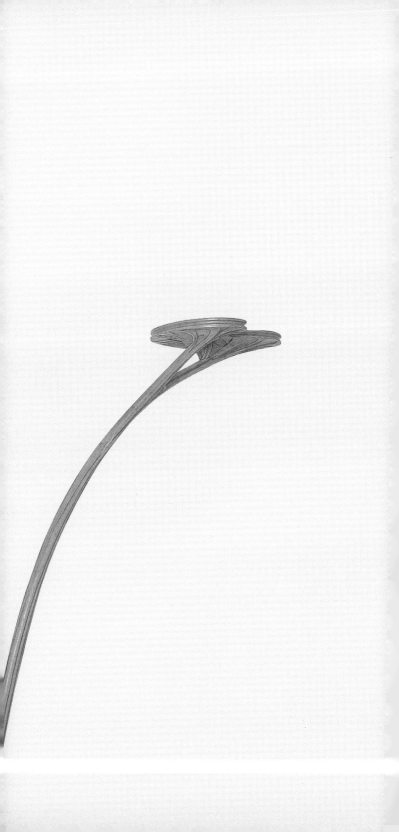

Art Nouveau
1889–1905

Buffet

HECTOR GUIMARD, 1899/1900
Cherry wood with brass fittings and glass
Height 274 cm; inv. no. 83-001
Acquired with funds from the
Senatsverwaltung für
Kulturelle Angelegenheiten

Hector Guimard (1867–1942) is
considered one of the major architects
and all-round designers of French Art
Nouveau. Influenced by the filigree patterns
of Gothic art, which became popular
towards the end of the 19th century thanks
to Viollet-le-Duc and the enthusiasm for
nature of early Art Nouveau, which sought
inspiration in the structure of plants, he
designed extravagantly curvaceous flower
sculptures that are still a prominent feature
of the urban landscape of Paris. He it was
who designed the cast-iron entrances to the
first metro stations in time for the world
exhibition in 1900.

The buffet with the water lily leaves and
stems was designed for the Castel Henriette
villa in Sèvres. The dynamic language of
natural shapes is again the model for
Guimard here. The plant patterns develop
out of the body of the buffet in vertical,
organic curves. This asymmetrically
designed piece of furniture almost seems
like a plant sculpture. The choice of cherry
wood, too, sets it wholly apart from
the heavy, imitative furniture styles of
historicism.

The restless linearity also extends to the
darting details of the appliqué work—a
seismic expression of artistic sensibility
and restlessness around the turn of the
century. *IB*

13

Vase with chrysanthemum decoration and stand

FRANÇOIS EUGÈNE ROUSSEAU, c. 1884
Appert Frères, Paris
Flashed glass, cut and engraved
Height 17.7 cm; inv. no. 03-001
Gift of Dr. Margrit Bröhan

Eugène Rousseau (1827–1891) was a pioneer of *japonisme*.
The son of a Parisian crafts manufacturer, he came to public
notice at the Paris world exhibition in 1867 with a pottery service
painted with decorative motifs taken from Japanese coloured
woodcuts. Rousseau began designing glassware the same year,
collaborating with the Parisian glass manufactory Appert Frères.
He had great success with his thick-walled glassware inspired by
Chinese cut stones, which he exhibited at an exhibition of arts
and crafts in Paris in 1884. The vase dates from this period.
Marked resonances of Asian art are evident not only in the
stylised chrysanthemum decoration but also in the stand,
which underlines the artistic nature of the vessel. Rousseau's
work had some influence on Nancy glassmaker Emile Gallé. *CK*

Vase with moth

EMILE GALLÉ, Nancy, *c.* 1898
Flashed glass with fusions and metal foil inclusions, cut
Height 18.5 cm; inv. no. 75-013

Like many of his contemporaries, Nancy-based Emile Gallé (1846–
1904) was an enthusiastic disciple of East Asian art.
Of particular importance for him was his friendship with the
Japanese natural scientist and draughtsman Tokouso Takasuima,
who was in Nancy from 1885 to 1888 for study purposes.
Gallé developed a glass style of his own known as the Gallé genre,
which drew on many different influences and indeed became
emblematic of Art Nouveau in Lorraine. It combined decoration
and technology, nature motifs and colour effects in a way that
was wholly new to the art fashion of the time. All symmetry and
regularity was dispensed with. Gallé's view of nature was strongly
coloured by his interest in botany. He sought to capture mood,
using the play of
colour and light
that only glass
could offer.
A particular colour
effect is achieved
in this vase through
the metal foil over-
laid with green
glass. *CK*

Vase

EMILE GALLÉ, Nancy, 1900
Flashed glass with fusions (marquetry technique), cut
Height 14 cm; inv. no. 75-020

This vase is signed by the artist, with the addition *Gallé Etude 1900*. It is thus a technical experimental piece. The multi-layer flashing, which involved repeated heating and cooling, required countless experiments, during which many pieces were broken. To illustrate this to the public, at the world exhibition in Paris in 1900 Gallé set up a kiln surrounded by broken glass on his stand.

Both technically and in its motifs, the vase is a good example of the 'Gallé genre'. The lotus blossom was fused on separately. The process involved was patented by Gallé in 1898 under the name *marqueterie de verre* (glass marquetry). Presumably the idea came to him when he was doing designs for marquetry furniture and saw that the technique could be applied to the qualities of glass. The lotus plant—in Japanese iconography a symbol of purity—rises gleaming from the brownish background, suggesting watery depths.   *CK*

Decorative plate with iris in the moonlight

MARIANNE HØST, 1889
Den Kongelige Porcelainsfabrik, Copenhagen
Porcelain with underglaze painting
Diameter 39.5 cm; inv. no. 86-273

Under the direction of art director Arnold Krog (1856–1931), the Royal Porcelain Manufactory in Copenhagen attained a reputation as one of the leading porcelain manufacturers in Europe. Copenhagen ware became synonymous with modern design and new decorative styles. The systematic introduction of underglaze painting—a vital element in flat, stylised designs—was one major factor in this. The other was the reduction of tones to delicate blue, grey and green that this necessarily involved. The pictorial motifs chosen manifest the influence of *japonisme*, the adaptation of East Asian motifs in a western context. Krog was one of the great pioneers of Art Nouveau porcelain. The enthusiasm with which the *japoniste* motifs and forms were adopted indicates his receptiveness towards modern art fashions. Originally trained as a painter, he had acquired his knowledge of this stylistic repertoire from studying Japanese woodcuts at dealer Siegfried (Samuel) Bing's gallery in Paris, which specialised in East Asian art. Marianne Høst (1865–1943) had been a close colleague of Krog since 1885, and she it was who painted this composition of an iris against the flat orb of the moon reflected in the water as an early example of *japonisme* in porcelain. The asymmetrical composition and strong stylisation are the technical features that reveal the Japanese influence, as does the choice of the iris motif. As in Europe, irises were rich in symbolism. They were admired as one of the 'four noble plants' and therefore often depicted in art. *IB*

'Corvi Noctis' (Night Ravens) tapestry

WALTER LEISTIKOW, 1897/98
Wool, tapestry weave
Length 180 cm, width 180 cm; inv. no. 93-910
Acquired with funds from the
Stiftung Deutsche Klassenlotterie, Berlin

Landscape painter Walter Leistikow (1865–1908), a founding member of the Berlin Secession set up in 1898, also worked occasionally as a designer of handicraft items. He originally developed the motif of the night raven as a drawing for a decorative border for *Pan* periodical in 1896, but later worked it up into an independent large format. A keen traveller in Nordic countries, Leistikow shows here a nocturnal fjord landscape in the light of the moon, with the black silhouettes of ravens in the foreground. The water and cliffs are rendered in stylised, abstract form—the busy tracery of lines intensifies the eerie atmosphere of the scene. The Latin title is integrated into the border frame in almost symbolic form, drawing attention to the ancient, magic interdependence of writing and ornament.

Ravens have a strong symbolic meaning in a wide range of cultures. In myth, fairy tales and popular belief they are considered to be divine messengers, harbingers of misfortune or personifications of evil. The ambiguous, multi-level content of this scene suited the symbolist mood of *fin-de-siècle* art, which favoured the darkness of the abyss and the anti-rational. *IB*

Vase with iris leaves and flowers

ALBERT KLEIN, 1899
Königliche Porzellanmanufaktur, Berlin
Porcelain with flow glaze
Height 61.5 cm; inv. no. 85-112

At the world fair in Paris in 1900, Berlin's Royal Porcelain Manu-factory (KPM) set out to impress with an ostentatious programme. Among the few pieces that matched the new, organic approach to design was this large vase with three-dimensional irises, which were made from a particularly malleable porcelain mixture. Named Heinecke Mixture after its inventor Dr Albert Heinecke, the technical director of the KPM, it was a vital component in the production of a series of highly elaborate porcelain pieces produced by KPM around 1900.

Irises were among the favourite plants of Art Nouveau, becoming almost emblematic of the new style. The distinctive flowers and vertical orientation of the stems were easily converted into abstract or symbolic shapes, and were therefore ideally suited to the artistic ambitions of Art Nouveau. The symbolic meanings of the flower—in Greek mythology Iris was the goddess of the rainbow and messenger of the gods, and the flower has been important since antiquity in folklore, medicine and magic—could be considered arcane knowledge, and in its variable interpretations perfectly matched Art Nouveau's love of fluctuating concepts. *IB*

'Pavots et Étoiles' Vase (poppies and stars)

DAUM FRÈRES, Nancy / Maison Cardeilhac, Paris, c. 1897
Flashed glass, cut, silver
Height 26.6 cm; inv. no. 03-002
Gift of Dr. Margrit Bröhan

Encouraged by Gallé's success at the world fair in Paris in 1889, the second major glass manufacturer in Nancy, Daum Frères, also switched production from utility products to art glass. At first they kept to Gallé-style floral flashed glass, but soon developed techniques and decorations of their own.

The poppy depicted on the vase combined with the stars, and the dark violet coloration symbolises the worlds of dreams and the night. The silver mounting with its stalk-like supports cleverly picks up the decoration of the glass vase. The piece was made by the long-established Parisian silversmiths Cardeilhac. During the Art Nouveau period, stands and mountings were particularly popular for glass and ceramic objects. The symbiosis of vessel and stand was inspired by East Asian crafts. In Europe there was also a tradition dating back to mediaeval times of enhancing valuable vessels with mounts made of precious metals. *CK*

Woman torch-bearer
from the 'Jeu de l'écharpe' centrepiece

AGATHON LÉONARD, 1899
Manufacture Nationale de Porcelaine, Sèvres
Biscuit ware
Height 56 cm, inv. no. 96-029

At the world fair in Paris in 1900, the porcelain factory in Sèvres scored a great success with a fifteen-piece *surtour de table*, a festive table decoration that consisted of twelve dancers and two women holding torches, plus a female flute-player. In the design of his figures, sculptor Agathon Léonard (1841–1923) drew his inspiration from modern expressive dance and the classical fashion of his time. In their graceful movements, the dancers are related to

each other in a strict choreography. The two torch-bearers and the flute-player were conceived as plinth-based figures in the original exhibition, where they constituted a statuesque counterpoint to the lively dance of the other figures. The hieratic pose of the torch-bearer enables the robe to be given a rather complex treatment that is almost an anticipation of the famous Delphos clothes of Italian designer Mariano Fortuny, first produced in 1905. *IB*

'Five Swans' tapestry

OTTO ECKMANN, 1896/97
Kunstwebschule Scherrebek
Wool, tapestry weave
Length 235 cm, width 75 cm; inv. no. 93-911
Acquired with funds from the
Stiftung Deutsche Klassenlotterie, Berlin

The art weavers' college at Scherrebek (now Skærbæk, Denmark) was founded in 1896 in the wake of the *fin-de-siècle* art reform movement. Particularly in the countries of northern Europe, there was a new enthusiasm for textile art. Tapestries reached high artistic standards and became outstandingly important as an integral component of interior design. Around 1894, Otto Eckmann (1865–1902), who was originally a painter, resolutely put down his brushes in favour of applied art—a decision that was taken by numerous artists of the generation around 1900. The aesthetic design of the totality of solid objects proved to have greater appeal than the specialised field of painting. Eckmann became famous as a designer not only of book art and typography, but also of furniture and metal items.

The *Swans* tapestry—one of the most successful designs of the weaving college at Scherrebek—combines modern design princip-les with East Asian influences, a combination that would prove to be one of the principal artistic currents of the Art Nouveau movement. Abstraction, stylisation and aesthetic priorities were borrowed from Japanese art. In this case, Eckmann even went so far as to adapt the tall, narrow format of a Japanese *kakemon* (roll picture). *IB*

Art Nouveau 1889–1905

Déjeuner (breakfast service) with crocus decoration

KONRAD HENTSCHEL, 1896
Kgl. Porzellanmanufaktur, Meissen
Porcelain with underglaze painting
inv. no. 77-444

Floral abstraction and vertical orientation in ornament and shape
are the features that distinguish the first Art Nouveau service
produced by the old-established German company. It was in
Meissen in 1708/10 that Johann Böttger succeeded in producing
porcelain in Europe for the first time. The flowering of this manufactory coincided with the Rococo style in art, and the styles then
evolved still play a part in the company's range.

Around 1900, however, modern styles featured prominently in
production. This little breakfast service was exhibited at the world
exhibition in Paris in 1900, where it was a great success. Konrad
Hentschel was a modeller in the factory, and came from a family
with many ties to Meissen. His brother Rudolf Hentschel worked
as a painter, while his father Julius Hentschel was considered
one of the great *pâte-sur-pâte* specialists. *IB*

Centrepiece with water lilies

PER ALGOT ERIKSSON, *c.* 1900
Rörstrand's Porslinsfabriker AB, Stockholm
Porcelain with underglaze painting
Height 29 cm; inv. no. 92-045

Sweden played a considerable part in the international artistic
debate associated with the reform movement around 1900, thanks
to the output of the Rörstrand porcelain factory in Stockholm. The
factory's artistic director was the painter and versatile handicrafts
designer Alf Wallander (1862–1914). Under his artistic aegis,
he firm developed a special style of porcelain that was shown at
the major exhibitions of the day – particularly in Germany – to great
acclaim. A characteristic of the new porcelain creations was the
rendering of plant decoration in relief or the three-dimensional
form of flowers and plants. The delicate coloration of the blue and
green tones gives these one-off pieces an especially delicate and
decorative look.
The large, depressed baluster pot is a graceful representation of
an underwater world. The large, open bloom of the water lily is
developed in three dimensions, like the typical leaves and buds
resting on the shoulder of the vase, while the roots and stems that
reach down into the depths of the water are shaped in light relief
in the delicate range of blue tones of the water. *IB*

Water jug from a washing set

Metallwarenfabrik J. P. Kayser & Sohn, Krefeld, *c.* 1901
Pewter, cast
Height 35.5 cm; inv. no. 77-099

Utensils made of pewter, brass and copper have a tradition in
Europe going back to the Middle Ages. During the Art Nouveau
period the tradition was revisited and revived with new forms of
ornamentation.
A particularly characteristic example of the phenomenon was
Krefeld-based company Kayser & Sohn, which had a notable
success at the Paris world fair in 1900. Its softly modelled utensils
largely dispensed with historic ornamentation, and thereby
made a substantial contribution to the spread of modern pewter.
Kayser pewter also represented a technical innovation. In a further
development of Britannia metal, the lead content was replaced
by antimony and copper, so that the pewter did not oxidise so
quickly and gained a matt, silvery sheen.
The almost sculptural-looking vessel is a good example of the
extensive collection of Kayser pewter in the Bröhan Museum.
The relief decoration shows motifs of marine creatures and plants.
The washing set includes a similarly decorated basin. *CK*

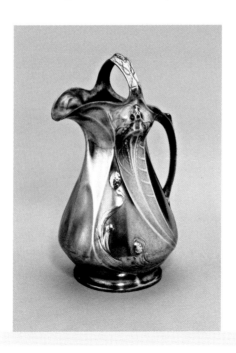

Fish service (no. 688 with decoration 624)

HERMANN GRADL, 1899/1900
Kgl. Bayerische Porzellanmanufaktur, Nymphenburg
Porcelain with overglaze painting
inv. no. 77-538

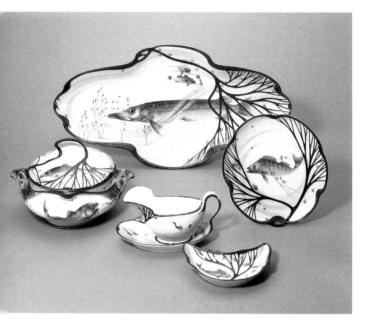

In 1898 Hermann Gradl (1869–1934), a landscape painter of
the Munich School, gave up painting in favour of the design of
applied art objects. He began working for the Nymphenburg
manufactory around 1899, the co-operation continuing until 1905.
This service decorated with a variety of fish shows not only water
creatures but also aquatic plants in a naturalistic but nonetheless
thoroughly modern fashion. In their organic outline, the design of
the individual pieces delightfully synthesises shape and decoration—
the brown algae form a graphic motif and grow out of the surface in
three-dimensional form as the framing and handles. In this elaborate
service, Gradl's inspiration was obviously Félix Braquemond's so-
called Rousseau service. *IB*

Iris vase, with lid

Haagsche Plateelbakkerij, Rozenburg/The Hague, 1903
Eggshell porcelain with overglaze painting
Height 62 cm; inv. no. 75-513

The Rozenburg Porcelain Factory in Rozenburg, a suburb of The Hague, was founded in 1883, but it did not gain a reputation as a manufactory of artistic distinction until more than a decade later, in 1895, when Juriaan Kock was appointed director. The Hague became a centre of Art Nouveau in painting style, influenced by the floral abstractions of the French and by Japanese decorative elements, and noted for the use of exclusive materials. The shape and decorative style of this tall vase — it is astonishingly light as a result of its extremely thin-walled porcelain — with iris motifs were in line with international trends in Art Nouveau. Eggshell porcelain had been produced since 1899, and had been an immediate hit with the art world. The artificial character of such objects, evident in the highly sophisticated, delicate material and the sensitive painting, satisfied a longing for aesthetic alternative worlds remote from ordinary pragmatism. *IB*

Vase with Phänomen decoration

FRANZ HOFSTÄTTER (?), 1900
Glasfabrik Joh. Loetz Witwe, Klostermühle
Colourless glass with opal glass flashing, thread fusions,
reduced and iridescent
Height 20.9 cm; inv. no. 75-067

The appeal of the vase lies in the silvery gleam of the surface,
reminiscent of water effects. Phänomen decoration was obtained
by braiding the glass with a variety of glass containing silver or
tin and subsequently blowing into a ribbed form. Following the
appearance of the glass style produced by American glassmaker
Louis Comfort Tiffany, Loetz Witwe promoted its Phänomen
products as 'Tiffany-type' works, though at lower prices than the
American originals. Independently of Tiffany, the southern Bohemian
glass factory had developed numerous special techniques for
producing lustre glass and registered patents for them.
The Phänomen-decorated vase is among the rare Loetz pieces
to be signed. It was designed for the Paris world exhibition in
1900. The firm's range of glass shimmering in all colours of the
rainbow scored a notable success with the public and was widely
bought, making a substantial contribution to the popularity of
Art Nouveau glass. *CK*

Decorative plate

CLÉMENT MASSIER, Golfe Juan, *c.* 1900
Faïence with lustre decoration
Diameter 36.4 cm; inv. no. 75-470

From 1889
Clément Massier
(1845–1917), born
of an old-established family
of potters, followed the fashions
of the day in his ceramics with iridescent, gleaming lustre glazes.
Massier's work introduced the technique of lustre glazes to France.
At the world exhibition in Paris in 1900 he won a gold medal.
Inspiration for these special glazes came from exotic sources such
as ceramic pieces from the Islamic countries or archaeological
excavations of ancient glass and pottery, which had acquired an
iridescent surface layer due to chemical reaction with the soil. Tiffany
and Loetz glassware attained worldwide fame with coloured lustre
decoration. The iridescence, ornamentation and enigmatic quality
of these pieces were what made them so appealing. They were
particularly in sympathy with the mental and emotional world of Art
Nouveau. In their abstract, coloured beauty the ornamentation of
the pieces also paved the way for a reception of modern art. The
contemporaneous fashion for Impressionist painting showed a
similar readiness to abandon realistic representation. *IB*

Vase with sculptural imitations of precious stones and spider's web decoration

Keramikwerke Amphora, Turn-Teplitz, *c.* 1900
Faïence with enamel and gold (so-called 'jewel porcelain')
Height 22.5 cm; inv. no. 75-404

When the Amphora factory in northern Bohemia entered the market in 1895, it was with a range of most unusual ceramic pieces. The luxuriant plant ornamentation, coloured flow glazes, sculptural beasts as decoration and enamel and gold ornament revealed all the ambivalence of the turn of the century—the opulence of the outgoing 19th century combined with the modern, plant-line and organic beauty of Art Nouveau.

The 'jewel porcelain' style owes much to the search for precious stones then popular in the forests and hills of Bohemia—the immanent gleams of an already romantic landscape found an artificial (and artistic) counterpart in the preference for coloured stones and glass.

The impressed cavities in the material of the vase express the amorphousness of shape that was considered ideal in 'living materials'. *IB*

Art Nouveau 1889–1905

Furniture suite (so-called 'Uccle furniture')

HENRY VAN DE VELDE, *c.* 1895
Bubinga wood, chairs with rush seats
inv. no. 89-924
Acquired with funds from the
Stiftung Deutsche Klassenlotterie, Berlin

Henry van de Velde (1863–1957) was
undoubtedly one of the great all-round
artists of the 20th century. He initiated a
renaissance in the applied arts, not only in
a formal sense but also in a spiritual and
philosophical respect.

After a successful career as a painter,
around 1892 he suffered something of
an identity crisis, and gave up painting.
Two years later, around 1894/95, without
any architectural training he started work
building himself a house in Uccle, a
suburb of Brussels. From the external
architecture down to the smallest piece
of furnishing inside, van de Velde
designed a domestic cosmos at *Villa
Bloemenwerf* that accorded with his
idea of the reconciliation of art and life.
The furnishings combine elements of
rural Flemish tradition with the trends in
new art around 1900—a combination
that, in introducing a national tradition,
was wholly in the international spirit of the
new stylistic fashion.

In his strict stylisation and reduction to
essentials, Van de Velde proved himself
an innovator, taking up the dynamic
structure of Art Nouveau in its purest
form and stringently implementing it.
He applied his principle—'line is a force'—
in many ways. The Uccle chair is considered a classic design, and was produced
by him in a number of variants. *IB*

Art Nouveau 1889–1905

Pair of candelabra

HENRY VAN DE VELDE, 1898/1899
Silver-plated bronze
Height 58.5 cm; inv. no. 89-901
Acquired with funds from
the Stiftung Deutsche Klassenlotterie, Berlin

Henry van de Velde made line the sole expressive element of his designs—an artistic principle that was a radical rejection of the decorative ballast of the late 19th century and led to a reassessment of applied art. The soft, fluid lines are here the principal feature of the design, well-suited to the living, moving light of the candles it was designed to hold. The candelabrum belongs to the important early designs by van de Velde. As it is not pure silver, the material is not costly, and yet it is one of the most expensive pieces that van de Velde produced and sold at this time.

One of the purchasers was his friend, patron and best client, Harry, Count Kessler, whose apartment in Berlin was redesigned by van de Velde in the same year. As an art writer, Kessler was a consistent champion of van de Velde's work. In his old age, he still expressed admiration for the spirit of *sérénité* that he found in van de Velde's creations (Diary, Brussels, 19th May 1930). *IB*

Floor vase from Villa Esche, Chemnitz

HENRY VAN DE VELDE, 1902
Steinzeugfabrik Reinhold Hanke, Höhr
Stoneware with ox-blood glaze
Height 59 cm; inv. no. 93-909

In 1902, Belgian artist Henry van de Velde moved from Berlin to
Weimar, where he was appointed consultant to the art industry
of Saxony-Weimar-Eisenach. For Van de Velde, who was interested
in all materials and the various branches of art, an appointment
of this kind was particularly appealing. A number of ceramic works
by him are known, like this large amphora vase. With its softly fluid,
organic structure, it demonstrates over a large surface the beauty
of living, flaming, veined ox-blood glazes. Because it was a softer
material to handle than porcelain, stoneware was favoured as a
material in ceramic art around 1900.

The Villa Esche was begun in 1903 for manufacturer Herbert
Esche. It was van de Velde's biggest architectural commission in
Germany. *IB*

Art Nouveau 1889–1905

Tea kettle with warmer, from a coffee and tea service

Orivit AG, Ehrenfeld, Cologne, c. 1903
Sterling silver
Height 39 cm; inv. no. 94-004

By the beginning of the 20th century, Cologne-based Orivit had become the principal rival of Kayser & Sohn. In 1898, the bronze-ware company registered the trade name Orivit for a particular type of tin alloy with a silvery gloss. Two years later the Orivit brandname became the company name.

Among its extensive range were decorative and utility ware made of non-precious and precious metals (pewter, copper, brass, silver) manufactured by industrial techniques. With its competitively priced products decorated in a floral Art Nouveau style, Orivit AG found a solid middle-class customer base. In 1905, the company was taken over by the Württembergische Metallwarenfabrik (WMF).

The tea kettle is part of a service that, with a few minor differences, was also made in pewter. *CK*

Bowl with spoon

CHARLES ROBERT ASHBEE, c. 1902
Guild of Handicraft Limited, London
Silver, green stone (probably chrysoprase), glass
Length 18.3 cm (bowl with handle), 14.6 cm (spoon);
inv. no. 90-057

What is impressive about this bowl is its plain elegance combined
with the unity of shape and decoration. The handle describes an
expansive curve, while stones and green glass provide delightful
colour highlights.

Charles Robert Ashbee (1863–1942) was among the leading
figures of the English Arts and Crafts movement. In 1888 he
founded the Guild of Handicraft, an arts and crafts workshop with
an attached school and shops in London. The aim was to have
the entire design, execution and distribution of the products
handled by a creative working community. Ashbee wanted to
counter specialisation and the industrial division of labour with
individuality and an identification with the whole process of manufacture. At its peak the Guild of Handicraft had a workforce of thirty.
In 1900 Ashbee and the Scottish artist couple Charles Rennie
Mackintosh and his wife Margaret Macdonald Mackintosh were
represented at the 8th Secession exhibition in Vienna. Their plain or
strongly geometricised designs were of fundamental importance
for the work of the Wiener Werkstätte. *CK*

Pair of candlesticks

JOSEPH MARIA OLBRICH, *c.* 1902
Eduard Hueck, Lüdenscheid
Pewter, cast, each candlestick being assembled
from two halves
Height 36 cm each; inv. no. 92-063

In the early 20th century there was collaboration between Austrian
architect and designer Joseph Maria Olbrich (1867–1908) and
Lüdenscheid-based metal manufacturers Eduard Hueck. This pair
of candlesticks designed by Olbrich combining flowing line and
abstract ornamentation is a good example of the geometricisation
of form that increasingly ousted the floral Art Nouveau style in
Germany around 1901.
Olbrich was in the vanguard of the development. A pupil of
Otto Wagner, he was a co-founder of the Viennese Secession
and designed its headquarters, the celebrated Secession building,
in 1898. A year later, he accepted the invitation of Grand Duke
Ernst Ludwig of Hessen-Darmstadt to join the Darmstadt Artists'
Colony. He and Peter Behrens became its leading figures,
designing not only numerous striking buildings, such as the Hoch-
zeitsturm (wedding tower) on the Mathildenhöhe by Olbrich,
but also furniture, metalwork and other handicraft pieces. *CK*

Art Nouveau 1889–1905

The so-called 'Wertheim Room':
buffet, extendable table with six chairs

PETER BEHRENS, 1902
Möbelschreinerei Anton Blüggl, Berlin
Stained oak, slate, glass
Height of buffet 190.5 cm; inv. no. 98-022

Other objects:
porcelain service, glasses and silver to designs by
PETER BEHRENS (between 1900 and 1930);
carpet by OTTO ECKMANN/Krefelder Teppichfabrik AG, 1898

Peter Behrens (1868–1940) attained a
decicive point in his artistic development as
a member of the 'Darmstadt Seven', who
were the most influential group in the colony
of artists at Mathildenhöhe around 1900.
In 1902 he built himself a house there, an
important and significant building for the
new reform movement in Germany.
In this, as a painter, architect and designer
of handicrafts, he achieved a synthesis
of all artistic forms of expression, but it represented the end of the road for that
particular aspect of his own work.
Participation in the 'Modern Living Interiors'
exhibition at Wertheim's store in Berlin,
which accorded with his notion of a
'utilitarian luxury art that is affordable for
everyone' was the way forward for him.
Wertheim's store in Leipziger Strasse, an
element of the urban landscape in its new
building by Alfred Messel with ambitions for
further innovations, organised the exhibition
to promote an everyday aesthetic no longer
aimed solely at the tastes of the elite but
also in keeping with the times.
For Peter Behrens, the Wertheim Room
was the start of an outstanding career as an
industrial designer. In 1907, he joined forces
with AEG electricity company—a momentous
decision that led to his becoming one of
the leading designers for industry and architecture in modern industry. *IB*

Interim Period
1905–1920

Pair of candlesticks

CARL STOCK (designer), ADOLPH AMBERG (modeller),
c. 1904
Peter Bruckmann & Söhne, Heilbronn
Silver
Height 44 cm each; inv. no. 90-021

This pair of candlesticks, which was also obtainable in an electrical version, derives from a design by sculptor Carl Stock (1876–1945).

A conspicuous feature is the design of the branches in the shape of water lilies. Though this is a motif in the floral Art Nouveau vein, the jagged outline of the piece as a whole has moved on beyond that.

The manufacturer was the distinguished Heilbronn-based silverware firm of Peter Bruckmann & Söhne. Around the turn of the century, the company had a workforce of 650. It was a sign of its artistic ambitions that the firm took part in all major arts and crafts exhibitions. It had been run since 1886 by Peter Bruckmann (1865–1937), who himself had been to the arts and crafts school in Munich. By bringing in external artists he modernised the product range and abandoned eclectic historic styles. *CK*

Interim Period 1905–1920

Putto with flower garland (Spring)

EMIL MEIER, c. 1906
Wiener Keramik, Vienna
Faïence, painted
Height 38.5 cm; inv. no. 75-571

Though the Wiener Werkstätte had a pottery workshop from 1917,
art ceramics had been important even before that. The link was
Michael Powolny (1871–1954), who studied at the Arts and Crafts
College in Vienna and was considered a founder of the Viennese
Secession. In 1905, he and Gerhard Löffler founded 'Wiener
Keramik', whose products were distributed by the Wiener Werkstätte
from 1907. Many of the designs were by Powolny himself, but a
number of models are by other artists such as the potter Emil Meier.
Though the subject of the putto through the four seasons is basically
derived from Baroque garden sculpture, the stylised reproduction
of cascading flowers and the reduced colour palette follow modern
design principles. Austrian ceramics made something of a speciality
of combining tradition and modernism at this time. Like the putti,
another range that enjoyed great popularity were the neo-Biedermeier 'crinoline figurines'. *CK*

'Pierrot and Pierrette' group (carnival couple)

JOSEPH WACKERLE, 1909/10
Kgl. Bayerische Porzellanmanufaktur, Nymphenburg
Porcelain with underglaze painting
Height 33 cm; inv. no. 77-542

One of the most important designers of porcelain was Joseph Wackerle (1880–1959), who trained as a sculptor and graphic artist and did outstanding figurines for Nymphenburg and Berlin. This figurine group shows typical characters from the *commedia dell'arte*, misleadingly labelled *Pierrot and Pierrette*. With their standardised costumes the protagonists can be precisely identified, but this does not match the name given them. The male figure is Harlequin, whose costume traditionally consists of a mask and diamond-patterned costume. The female companion to Harlequin is Columbine, whose dress is normally more coquettish and seductive. Perhaps what we have here is only in fact one of the numerous ancillary female figures of the *commedia dell'arte*, who confers an erotic, symbolic charge to the representation with the birdcage she is carrying. In contrast, the

unhappy lover Pierrot of the title is traditionally dressed in white, often with overlong sleeves, and is quite the opposite of the victorious, self-assured lover Harlequin. A letter from Wackerle to the first purchaser of the group, Carl Stern, indicates that the sculptor was fully familiar with Italian comedy. He describes the figure correctly as 'Harlequin.' *IB*

Buffet

BRUNO PAUL, 1906/07
Vereinigte Werkstätten, Munich
Stained oak with inlays, brass hardware, glass
Height 209 cm; inv. no. 95-025

1906 was a key year for Bruno Paul (1874–
1968). His participation in the
Third German Arts and Crafts Exhibition in
Dresden had secured his reputation as one
of the leading German designers. Previously
a graphic artist for the satirical review
Simplicissimus, he had already won a gold
medal for his furniture in Paris in 1900.
No doubt thanks to his success with a
dining room interior in Dresden, he was
appointed head of the Berlin art and crafts
museum school in the same year. From an
early stage Bruno Paul's designs manifested
a range of austere forms based on basically
geometrical patterns. They are good
examples of the cool modernity that took
institutional form in the principles of the
Deutscher Werkbund, founded in Berlin
in 1907. *IB*

A group of wine glasses

OTTO PRUTSCHER, *c*. 1907
Meyr's Neffe, Adolf (execution), E. Bakalowitz & Söhne (sales)
Colourless glass, flashed dark red and cut
Height 20.9 cm; inv. no. 75-334; 75-335; 98-017

The strictly geometric decoration and clear structure make the wine glasses typical examples of the early, very reduced style of the Wiener Werkstätte. Architect Otto Prutscher (1880–1949) was a pupil of Josef Hoffmann and an employee of the Wiener Werkstätte. His work in glass resulted in particularly original and successful designs. The group of cut wine glasses with geometrical decoration was done in 1907 as a commission for Viennese glass retailers E. Bakalowitz & Söhne, who maintained close contacts with modern-minded artists of the Viennese arts and crafts school and the Wiener Werkstätte. The glasses were made by the southern Bohemian firm of Meyr's Neffe at Adolf, in Winterberg. The radicalism of the design heralded the end of the floral style of Art Nouveau. *CK*

'Merkur' coffee service

JOSEF HOFFMANN, 1910
Pfeiffer & Löwenstein, Schlackenwerth
Wiener Porzellanmanufaktur Josef Böck
for the Wiener Werkstätte
inv. no. 95-927

After training as an architect, Josef Hoffmann (1870–1956)
developed into one of Viennese modernism's most prominent
figures. At his instigation the Wiener Werkstätte, an association based
on the reformist ideas of the English Arts and Crafts movement
workshops, was founded in 1903. With his linear, abstract geometrical forms and ornamentation Hoffmann succeeded in creating
a distinctive style of his own within the international Art Nouveau
movement. It was moreover a style that could hold its own in the
modernism of the following decades.
The slightly convex shapes of the vessels still suggest a persistence
of the organic style, but the austere, ceremonious black and gold
decoration is a typical product of the Viennese Secession.
The service was produced for the Wiener Werkstätte by Pfeifer &
Löwenstein in Schlackenwerth (Ostrov) — an example of the close
connection between Viennese modernism and the Bohemian
art industry. *IB*

Vase

KARL KLAUS, *c.* 1910
Porzellanfabrik Ernst Wahliss, Vienna
Faïence, overglaze and gold painting ('Serapis faïence')
Height 37.5 cm; inv. no. 75-565

With its simple shape, the vase provides a large surface for
decorative ornamentation. The scene depicted shows two girls
surrounded by flowers, one of them playing a flute, while the
other appears to be enjoying the splendour of the flowers.
The spring-like nature of the subject is in harmony with the
gleaming, gold-enhanced coloration. This intensity of colour was
a speciality of 'Serapis ware' (the name is derived from the
ancient Egyptian god of fertility). The range was launched by the
old-established Viennese pottery firm of Ernst Wahliss in 1911.
Art critics of the time noted the Serapis products with interest.
Parallels were made with oriental pottery and the clear colour
scale of Biedermeier porcelain.
The vase was designed by Karl Klaus, born in 1889, a pupil
of Josef Hoffmann, who like Hans Bolek and Otto Prutscher
worked for Wahliss. The strong outlines
and yet opulent style are reminiscent
of Klimt's imagery. *CK*

'Modern Pallas Athene' figurine

HERMANN HUBATSCH, 1911
Kgl. Porzellanmanufaktur, Berlin
Porcelain with underglaze painting
Height 34 cm; inv. no. 77-224

Around 1900 Pallas Athene, the formidable classical goddess
and guardian of science and art, was also awarded the job of
patron goddess of the Secession, i.e. modern, unacademic art.
This fashion figurine from the Berlin factory is an amusing take on
that. Pallas Athene's normal attributes such as a plumed helmet
and her sacred animal, the owl, feature as fashion accessories in
the form of a hat and handbag. She carries a lapdog, an ironic
comment on her supposedly warlike nature. Her fashionable outfit
includes a trouser dress of the kind with which Paul Poiret caused
such a stir when they first appeared around 1910 to howls of
outrage.
The latter-day Pallas Athene is thus an emancipated, fashionable
woman, fortified by education and extravagant fashions and ready
for the fray in the battle of the sexes. *IB*

'The Three Ice Saints' tapestry

JOHAN THORN PRIKKER, 1911
A. Pahde weavers, Krefeld
Wool, tapestry weave
Length 118 cm, width 173 cm; inv. no. 98-020

The words Pancratius, Mamertus and Servatius refer to three saints on whose successive feast days (11th to 13th May) popular belief predicts a bout of cold weather. Dutch artist Thorn Prikker renders this in an expressive and at the same time abstract fashion—St Mamertus crushes a grape as a sign of frost, St Pancras wears a fur hat. Crystalline shapes and jagged structures also conjure up associations of frost and ice.

Johan Thorn Prikker (1868–1932) taught from 1900 at the arts and crafts college in Krefeld, a town that thanks to the progressive director of the Kaiser Wilhelm Museum had a notable reputation. In 1909, Karl Ernst Osthaus, a powerful champion of modernism, brought Thorn Prikker to Hagen. The religiously ecstatic style that distinguishes Thorn Prikker's work is also featured in the large-scale glass and tempera pictures that he did for Osthaus's Folkwang Museum. *IB*

Sleeping Vagabonds
(Russian Peasant Couple Asleep)

ERNST BARLACH, 1912 (design), 1922 (execution)
Staatliche Porzellan-Manufaktur, Meissen
Böttger stoneware
Height 28 cm; inv. no. 77-471

In 1922 the sculptor Ernst Barlach (1870–1938) made the model
of the *Sleeping Vagabonds* for moulding in Böttger stoneware and
porcelain. The work was listed in the model book of the Meissen
porcelain company as *Russian Peasant Couple Asleep*. It was
based on a wooden sculpture that Barlach had already exhibited
in 1913 at the 'Berlin Secession'.

The use of Böttger stoneware gives the product a wholly individual
character. Because of its fine modelling characteristics and warm,
reddish-brown colour tones, the material is particularly suited
to modelling sculptural works. Max Adolf Pfeiffer, newly appointed
as director of the Meissen company in 1918, decided to re-adopt
Böttger stoneware as a production material. He also strengthened
collaboration with well-known artists. *CK*

Sideboard

PAUL THIERSCH, 1912
Möbelschreinerei Otto Jüdersleben
American walnut, glass
Height 153 cm; inv. no. 97-004
Acquired from the estate of Kurt and Sophie Hildebrandt, Berlin

Paul Thiersch (1879–1928) studied architecture before joining
Bruno Paul as office manager in 1907. In 1910, he worked with
Paul on the German contribution to the world fair in Brussels. In
Berlin, Thiersch also came into contact with associates of the writer
Stefan George. Through her brother, the doctor and philosopher
Kurt Hildebrandt, the painter Fanny Hildebrandt, whom Thiersch
later married, was particularly sympathetic to an outlook that aimed
to integrate the mental and spiritual world with the requirements of
everyday life. Thiersch consequently designed for the Hildebrandt
family a whole series of unusual pieces of furniture, whose unique
character is emphasised by an expressiveness of form. Until 1915,
Thiersch worked as a freelance architect, but was then appointed
director of Burg Giebichenstein arts and crafts school in Halle an der
Saale, which he reorganised to make it one of the leading centres
of the German art reform movement. *IB*

Bowl

GEORG JENSEN, 1912
Georg Jensen, Copenhagen
Silver
Height 17.5 cm; inv. no. 77-017

The works of Danish silversmith Georg Jensen (1866–1935) are a stylistic halfway house between Art Nouveau and Art Deco, with floral ornamentation and a stereometric reduction of form. A characteristic feature is that the ornamentation is confined to handles, supports or (as with this bowl) the stem. The stylised decorations in the shape of mistletoe leaves and berries make a distinctive contrast to the smooth surface of the body. Jensen's silver objects were produced only in small editions.

Jensen came from humble origins and worked hard to get a training. After studying sculpture at the academy in Copenhagen and making his first experiments in ceramics, in 1904 he opened a jewellery studio in Copenhagen, which by 1916 had become an expanding joint stock company. In later years, he stepped down from management, but continued to make designs. *CK*

'Ceres' dinner service
THEO SCHMUZ-BAUDISS, 1912
Kgl. Porzellanmanufaktur, Berlin
inv. no. 77-195

The jubilee service celebrating the 150th anniversary of the KPM (Royal Porcelain Manufactory) in 1913 was designed to reflect both tradition and modernity. The design by the artistic director of the KPM, Theo Schmuz-Baudiss (1859–1942), with a dominant white body offset by sparingly used polychrome painting lined out with gold, was just right for the occasion, with a synthesis of ceremonial opulence and Prussian simplicity. The design was called Ceres after the classical goddess of agriculture and the fruits of the field — visible as decoration in the wheat-ear borders. The cornucopias which recur as a design feature in every piece symbolise the blessings and abundance of the earth. *IB*

Cockatoo

EMIL POTTNER, c. 1911
Majolika-Manufaktur, Karlsruhe
Earthenware, cast, painted, colourless lead glaze
Height 56 cm; inv. no. 75-462

The Karlsruhe company of Majolika-Manufaktur was founded in 1901, and still exists. Though the original initiative came from painter Hans Thoma and potter Wilhelm Süs, the first proprietor was Grand Duke Frederick I of Baden. The high-quality utensils and decorative objects were based on artists' designs, and were intended to meet demand from a wide range of customers, while at the same time moulding their taste. From 1910, production focused on ceramics for the building industry and bric-à-brac, where serial casting processes were used in the manufacturing process. This cockatoo, a naturalistic, lifesize design, is a serial product, though the painting was done by hand. The design was by painter and ceramicist Emil Pottner (1872–1942), who was based in Berlin from 1903 and was a member of the 'Berlin Secession'. In 1911, he supplied a number of animal models to Majolika in Karlsruhe. *CK*

Goblet

JOSEF HOFFMANN (shape of glass),
FELICE RIX (decoration), c. 1915/17
Wiener Werkstätte / Joh. Oertel & Co., Haida
Colourless glass, matt, incised and painted
Height 20.9 cm; inv. no. 75-339

Founded in 1903 by Josef Hoffmann and others, the Wiener
Werkstätte sold glass under its own name only from 1915 on,
collaborating with glass manufacturers such as Loetz Witwe,
Meyr's Neffe, Oertel and later Moser in Karlsbad. Most of the
designs were provided by Hoffmann (1870–1956) himself, like
this plain, stylistically slightly eclectic goblet. The Bohemian
firm of Joh. Oertel in Haida (Novy Bor) was responsible for the
execution, and then passed the unfinished glass to the artist
studios of the Wiener Werkstätte for decoration.
The highly inventive decorations done in enamel painting or
incision were applied by various artists in the studios, such as
ceramicists Felice Rix, Vally Wieselthier and Hilda Jesser. The
decorative variant illustrated here is by Felice Rix (1893–1967).
The stylised flowers with matt white incisions form a delightful
contrast to the transparent, partly black-framed glass body. *CK*

Bowl

ALFRED WALTER, *c.* 1914
Fachschule für Glasindustrie Steinschönau
Colourless glass, etched matt silk on the outside,
black schwarzlot and gold painting
Height 26.3 cm; inv. no. 75-310

Unlike the floral decorative style of French Art Nouveau glass and
southern Bohemian lustre glass, from 1910 northern Bohemia
tended to follow in the footsteps of the 'Viennese Secession' style.
Linear ornaments and stylised, intricate flower motifs with echoes
of Biedermeier techniques of glass decoration played an important
part in this.
In 1910, the Imperial College for the Glass Industry in Steinschönau
(Kamenický Šenov) set up a drawing studio with the aim of
raising the artistic level of northern Bohemian glass craftsmanship.
The college worked closely with various glass firms on the spot.
Drawing professors included Adolf Beckert (1884–1929) and
Alfred Walter (1873–1915), who created a series of dense linear
ornamental designs that were implemented in a 'feather-drawing'
style. The latter was developed around 1914 by the Steinschönau
glass refiner Karl Massanetz (1890–1918), a pupil of Koloman
Moser and Michael Powolny in Vienna. *CK*

Tea set

FRITZ SCHMOLL GEN. EISENWERTH, 1913
Bruckmann & Söhne, Heilbronn
Silver, rare wood
inv. no. 91-045

The service consists of a 'tea machine' (a tea kettle with a little warmer), a teapot, a cream jug, a sugar bowl and a tray. The sugar bowl originally had a glass insert with palmette edging. The walls of the individual components display various floral ornaments. Made by the Heilbronn-based firm of Bruckmann to a design by the Munich sculptor Fritz Schmoll gen. Eisenwerth (1883–1963), the set sold very well. In its combination of modern, stylised ornaments with neo-Biedermeier and neoclassical elements, it obviously suited the taste of the time. As the designs by the artists of the Wiener Werkstätte or the Darmstadt Artists' Colony show, updated stylistic borrowings were very characteristic of the interim period between Art Nouveau and Art Deco. *CK*

Interim Period 1905–1920

Teapot

JOHAN ROHDE, 1919
Georg Jensen, Copenhagen
Silver, high-quality wood
Height 17.5 cm; inv. no. 95-023

The unusual design of the teapot derives from Danish painter and designer Johan Rohde (1856–1935), who was among the leading artists of Danish modernism. He began in 1903 with silverware designs, when he had a cutlery set made to his own design in the metal workshop of Mogens Ballin, which was run at the time by silversmith Georg Jensen. This brought him to the attention of Jensen, who made Rohde one of his closest collaborators when Jensen set up a workshop of his own. Although strongly similar to Jensen's designs in style, the silverwork of Rohde manifests a stronger tendency towards clear, basic shapes and reduced ornamentation. Rohde's designs were a substantial influence in shaping the profile of Jensen silverware. *CK*

Mandarin duck ('Urstück', special limited edition)

MAX ESSER, 1919
Staatliche Porzellanmanufaktur, Meissen
Porcelain with polychrome overglaze painting
Height 20 cm, inv. no. 77-525

Max Esser (1885–1945) was a friend and pupil of the well-known animal sculptor August Gaul, and continued his tradition of animal figures. When he made the acquaintance of Max Adolph Pfeiffer, later the director of the Meissen porcelain factory, he was introduced to porcelain design, which was a whole new world for an artist who had hitherto worked in bronze. In 1919, Esser signed a long-term contract with Meissen, and continued the high standards for the traditional genre of animal figurines at the manufactory. With past artists such as Johann Joachim Kändler creating its porcelain animal figurines, Meissen had enjoyed almost an artistic monopoly in the genre since the 18th century, and in taking on Esser found a modern, expressive style to continue the tradition. The term *Urstück* indicates a small, richly painted limited edition of the figurine, in this case eleven, the figure shown here being number four. *IB*

Chair (Bergère)

PAUL IRIBE, 1914
Varnished ebony with cotton velveteen upholstery
Height 70 cm; inv. no. 80-082

Elegant pieces of French Art Deco were among the core items
of the Bröhan collection. Opulence and sophistication in modern
interior furnishings were favoured in France more than in any
other country. Paul Iribe (1883–1935) was among the early
pioneers of Art Deco, the period when the organic, plant-like style
of Art Nouveau was abandoned and a clear, classic but at the
same time extravagant line was preferred. There are many facets
to Iribe's work. He had established a reputation as a graphic artist
and designer for stage sets and theatrical costumes before he
took up the applied arts around 1910. He turned his hand to
jewellery and metalwork, plus numerous designs for furniture.
In Iribe's view, furniture ought to reflect contemporary aesthetics,
and in fact his works already mirrored the *zeitgeist* that would
take definitive shape in the arts in the interwar years. *IB*

Interim Period 1905–1920

Art Deco and Functionalism
1920–1939

Lady's writing cabinet

Salon Dominique, Paris, c. 1922
Beech, apple wood within,
shagreen veneer, ivory inlays,
silver-plated hardware
Height 92 cm; inv. no. 80-049

This writing cabinet is a typical elegant small lady's piece produced by the furnishing workshop Dominique. This business was the creation of interior designer André Domin (1883–1962) and art writer Marcel Genevrière (1885–1963), who founded it in 1919. Their output is indicative of the opulent Art Deco work turned out not long after the end of World War I. Dominique took part in the major exhibitions of the 1920s such as the Salon d'Automne and the Société des Artistes Décorateurs (SAD). Most notably, it was represented in 1925 at the seminal Exposition Internationale des Arts Décoratifs et Industriels Modernes, which gave its name to the whole Art Deco style.

The use of costly and choice woods is typical of Dominique furniture, as is the use of shagreen, an exotic leather with striking pigmentation and a sensuous tactile texture. Shagreen (from Fr. *chagrin*, originally meaning rough polishing leather) made from the hide of sharks or rays has been used on furniture since the 18th century, especially by the French decorator Jean-Claude Galuchat. It is used as a veneer for small boxes such as tea caddies and knife boxes. *IB*

Art Deco and Functionalism 1920–1939

Carpet with abstract geometrical pattern

**Société DIM (Décoration Intérieure Moderne),
Paris 1925**
**Wool, length 297 cm, width 410 cm;
inv. no. 94-044**

Immediately after the end of World War I
a series of luxury furnishing businesses were
set up in Paris representing the new,
modern and elegant Art Deco style. In
1918, René Jouert and Georges Mouveau
established the Société DIM. Its programme
comprised modern furniture, lighting,
mirrors, carpets and fabrics, which displayed
the characteristic mixture of Constructivism
and exclusivity of the early Art Deco period.
This carpet, produced around 1925,
manifests the typical zigzag style that was
symptomatic of the Art Deco period—the
curves, organic shapes and floral linearity
of the preceding Art Nouveau style were
abandoned in favour of the zigzag and
broken lines and geometric shapes of
1920s modern art. The Société DIM was
one of the exhibitors at the international
crafts exhibition in 1925, having a hand
in the interior decoration of the pavilion
illustrating a French embassy abroad
(Ambassade de France à l'Étranger),
though it also had a showroom of its own.

IB

Art Deco and Functionalism 1920–1939

Female head

VALLY WIESELTHIER, 1920/21
Wiener Werkstätte, Vienna
Faïence, hollow, with intricate applications, painted
Height 44 cm; inv. no. 75-583

The collection in the Bröhan-Museum has three heads designed
for the Wiener Werkstätte by potter Vally Wieselthier (1895–1945).
Apart from this girl's head, there are others of a faun and a bacch-
ante. According to the register of models, these were ceramic
originals produced in a single or at most two copies.

Like many distinguished potters of her generation, Vally Wieselthier
studied at the arts and crafts college in Vienna, where Michael
Powolny, Koloman Moser and Josef Hoffmann were among her
teachers. From 1921, she ran a pottery of her own in Vienna. In
1929, she emigrated to New York.

Her works are notable for their delight in colour and inventiveness,
and are often taken as emblematic of the Roaring Twenties. She
herself commented in 1926: 'Terracottas have something serious,
even sublime about them. But I love glazes, perhaps because I
get a kick out of colourful and joyful things generally.' *CK*

Art Deco and Functionalism 1920–1939

Daphne Glass

ENA [EMMA HELENA] Rottenberg (design), *c.* 1925
AUGUST BISCHOF (?) / J. & L. Lobmeyr, Vienna-Steinschönau
Colourless glass, soft intaglio engraving, partly ground
Height 14.5 cm; inv. no. 84-055
Acquired with funds from the Museumsfonds der
Senatsverwaltung für Kulturelle Angelegenheiten

The glass is impressive in the delicacy of the decoration and
virtuosity of its execution. It depicts an episode from Greek
mythology, when Daphne is changed into a laurel. The designer
was Hungarian-born Ena Rottenberg (1893–1950), who studied
under Michael Powolny et al. at the Viennese arts and crafts college.
In the 1920s she collaborated with the Wiener Werkstätte, doing
designs for ceramics and ivory paintings. She also designed glass
decoration for Viennese glassware suppliers Lobmeyr. The
technical implementation of the Daphne motif was possibly the
work of August Bischof, who was among the most skilful glass
engravers from the Steinschönau area, and from 1910 worked
for Lobmeyr. *CK*

Vase with cockatoo

ADOLF FLAD (painting), 1923
Staatliche Porzellanmanufaktur, Berlin
Porcelain, overglaze painting
Height 59 cm; inv. no. 01-015
Gift of Dr. Margrit Bröhan

In contrast to the decorative style of Art Nouveau, which used
two-dimensional underglaze painting almost exclusively, there was
a return to overglaze painting in the 1920s, which enabled more
precise graphic tracing and interesting coloration. The lower firing
temperature of the porcelain permitted decorative effects, here
the magnificent harmony of black and gold effected in this large
vase produced by the Berlin factory. A leading light of the painting

department at the
factory from 1895
to 1932 was Adolf
Flad (1881–1937).
He was considered
one of the top
porcelain painters,
whose renderings of
tendrils, flowers and
animals were the
glory of the KPM's
reputation. Because
of their characteristic
plumage, cockatoos
were a favourite
animal motif in
applied art for three-
dimensional figures
or as decoration.
There are numerous
depictions of the bird
in both Art Nouveau
and Art Deco. *IB*

Table, mirror, standard lamp
EDGAR BRANDT, 1925
Wrought iron, marble, glass
Inv. nos. 83-007; 80-026: 80-027

Alsatian-born Edgar Brandt (1880–1960) was, along with
Jacques-Emile Ruhlmann and Jean Puiforcat, one of the most
important exponents of Art Deco in France.
The son of a machine manufacturer, he soon became familiar
with the raw material—iron—that he would later use as a principal
resource in his work. He was fascinated by iron, transforming its
roughness and weight with designs of filigree delicacy and unusual lightness. Around 1900, he launched his career with
handicraft works, but in later years he returned to his first love,
wrought iron, thoroughly approving the use of machinery in his
work. His attitude was that making contemporary pieces should
involve contemporary manufacturing processes, and in any case,
the latter often offered new artistic opportunities. Brandt's
business made gates, grilles, staircase balustrades, lift cages and
individual items for domestic interiors. A general feature that his
artistic designs share is a preference for abstract, stylised and
filigree decorative plant motifs in combination with heavy black
metal. The art objects of Edgar Brandt derive their peculiar charm
from the combination of two apparently incompatible qualities—
lightness and heaviness. *IB*

Art Deco and Functionalism 1920–1939

Vase with lid with stylised garlands and fish-scale ornamentation

HENRI RAPIN, 1926
Manufacture Nationale de Sèvres
Porcelain with overglaze painting
Height 26.5 cm; inv. no. 80-185

The next major challenge to the French Manufacture Nationale after its great success with Art Nouveau products at the world fair in Paris in 1900 was the international exhibition of modern arts and crafts in 1925. This precious, elegant porcelain piece with its delicate coloration was a prime exhibit, as it perfectly matched the tastes of the time. A typical feature of Art Deco was the use of gold within a colour composition. Henri Rapin, who was artistic director of Sèvres from 1920 to 1934, managed to induce leading handicraft designers to work for the factory, a good example being the distinguished cabinet-maker Jacques-Emile Ruhlmann. *IB*

La prière (The Prayer)
JEAN LAMBERT-RUCKI, 1932
Claude Valsuani Fondeurs, Paris
Bronze, patinated black, mounted on an oak base
Height 24 cm; inv. no. 81-325

The Polish painter and sculptor Jean Lambert-Rucki (1888–1967) lived in Paris from 1911, and the following year joined the 'Section d'Or' group of artists, whose members included Robert and Sonja Delaunay, Marcel Duchamp and Frank Kupka. In a fruitful exchange with the artistic avantgarde in Paris, Lambert-Rucki developed a style of his own that combines elements of Cubism, Constructivism and 'Primitivism'. From 1929, he exhibited at the 'Union des Artistes Modernes', an artists' association that numbered Le Corbusier, Pierre Chareau, Jean Puiforcat and Raymond Templier among its members.

This praying figure is representative of Lambert-Rucki's exploration of religious themes, which became a major feature of his post-1930 work. It impressively combines supplication, humility and repentance in the over-large hands joined in prayer and the kneeling posture. The figure is depersonalised, the message abstracted from the individual fate, thereby conferring on it a general validity. *CK*

Art Deco and Functionalism 1920–1939

Parts of a dining room
JACQUES-EMILE RUHLMANN, 1925/28
Cupboard macassar ebony, oak inside, doors with amboyna burl
veneer and ivory fillets; dining table amboyna grain knot veneer
and gilt brass; chairs mahogany with silver-plated metal shoes,
leather (replaced); inv. nos. 80-174; 80-181; 80-171

The work of Jacques-Emile Ruhlmann
must be ranked in the great craft tradition
of French *ébénistes*, the cabinet-makers
who had set standards in furniture-making
from the 18th century. At the great international modern crafts exhibition in Paris in
1925, Ruhlmann designed the 'collector's
house' (*hôtel d'un collectionneur*).
This pavilion, designing which enabled
Ruhlmann to indulge his skills as an
ensemblier, proved a key work in the
development of luxury Art Deco art in
France. Along with exotic woods such as
macassar ebony and *loupes d'amboine*
(amboyna burl), Ruhlmann used ivory,
tortoiseshell, mother of pearl and often
very expensive varnishes that gave his
classic, understated furniture the costly
elegance that his select and exclusive
clientele valued. These expensive furniture
pieces by Ruhlmann are to be seen in
four rooms at the Bröhan-Museum, forming
an internationally unique presentation of
this facet of French Art Deco. *IB*

Art Deco and Functionalism 1920–1939

Coffee and tea set

JEAN PUIFORCAT, pre-1926
Silver, ebony, silver-plated brass
inv. no. 88-384
Acquired with funds from the Stiftung
Deutsche Klassenlotterie, Berlin

The service with the electric samovar is typical for the cool,
logically worked out approach to design of the silversmith and
sculptor Jean Puiforcat (1897–1945). As the son of a silversmith,
he was thoroughly familiar with the tradition of silver craftwork,
but nonetheless gave historical styles and models a wide berth.
He was obsessed with mathematical calculations and proportional
relationships, and used the results in his designs. In 1925, he
took over the family workshop. At the big international exhibition
of arts and crafts in Paris in that year, he provided the silverware
for the 'Hôtel d'un Collectionneur' designed by Jacques-Emile
Ruhlmann, thereby coming to the attention of a specialist public.
Puiforcat combined minimalist shapes with elaborate handicraft manufacturing processes. His designs were produced in
small quantities and intended for an elite, modern-minded
clientele. *CK*

Cigarette cases

RAYMOND TEMPLIER, 1928/30
Silver, lacquered / shagreen / crushed eggshell
inv. no. 87-064; 87-160; 87-161
Acquired from casino surpluses, Berlin

These elegant cigarette cases were made by to designs jeweller
Raymond Templier (1891–1968), who worked for an old-
established family business in Paris, initially as an employee,
later as a co-proprietor. He had great success with his works at
the first post-World War I international exhibition of art and crafts,
the 'Exposition Internationale des Arts Décoratifs et Industriels
Modernes', which took place in Paris in 1925 and gave Art Deco
its name.

It was a time when fashion was turning away from organic Art
Nouveau in favour of severely reduced shapes combined with
decoration that was either abstract and futuristic or based on
stylised plant or figurative shapes. French art and crafts were
particularly noted for their use of luxurious materials and elaborate
craft execution.

The cigarette cases are typical examples of Art Deco with their
geometric decoration, well-chosen combination of materials and
colour, and elaborate production processes. *CK*

Art Deco and Functionalism 1920–1939

Vase with horses' heads (unique example)

ARISTIDE COLOTTE, 1930s
Colourless lead crystal glass, cut and chiselled
Height 17.3 cm, thickness of glass *c.* 2 cm;
inv. no. 75-002

This heavy vase by the French glass artist Aristide-Michel Colotte
(1885–1959) looks like a glass sculpture. After training as a jeweller
and engraver, Colotte ran his own glass workshop in Nancy. His
pieces are diametrically opposed in style and technique to the
colourful, richly nuanced Art Nouveau flashed glass of other artists in
Lorraine. Colotte learnt the techniques of glass cutting in the
workshops of Cristalleries de Baccarat, and developed a very
individual, technically highly intricate working method whereby
thick-walled glass objects not only underwent cutting and etching
but were also chiselled like sculptures. The motifs—often horses or
other animals, or abstract, Cubist-style ornamentation—derive a
good deal of their effect from the graphic interplay of light and
shadow. *CK*

Teapot

JEAN DESPRÉS, *c.* 1930
Pewter, wood, ivory
Height 12.8 cm; inv. no. 88-447

This futuristic teapot shows that its designer, Frenchman Jean Després (1889–1980), was in contact with the Cubists and also had an inclination for technology. After World War I, during which he worked as a fitter and technical draughtsman, he took over his father's handicraft business in Avallon in Burgundy. From the mid-1920s, he took part in exhibitions, initially anonymously, showing his avantgarde jewellery designs imbued with engineering aesthetics. He also did body pieces of pewter and silver.
The pewter surface of the teapot is produced by a hammering technique, which is in fact a typical process in silverwork. In this way Després signalled that it is not the value of the material but the artistic design that makes the uniqueness of an object. *CK*

Centrepiece

PAULA STRAUS, *c.* 1927
Peter Bruckmann & Söhne, Heilbronn
Silver
Height 21 cm; inv. no. 90-027

In the 1920s, cool modernist shapes appeared in the product range of the old-established Heilbronn-based firm Bruckmann & Söhne. A good many of these came from goldsmith Paula Straus (1893–1943), who had her own studio in the company. This centrepiece she designed about 1927 consists of two more or less hemispherical shapes. The handles are shaped as circular hoops with garlands of grapes, and form a delightful contrast to the smooth surface of the body of the work.
Paula Straus was a pupil of Paul Haustein's master classes at the arts and crafts school in Stuttgart. Subsequently she worked as a goldsmith and assistant professor. She was among the most gifted representatives of her guild. The Nazi terror regime brought her highly successful career to a brutal end. As Jews, she and her mother were deported to the concentration camps of Theresienstadt and Auschwitz and murdered there in 1943.
CK

Art Deco and Functionalism 1920–1939

Mocha set

MARGARETE HEYMANN-MARKS, c. 1929
Haël-Werkstätten für künstlerische Keramik,
Marwitz near Velten
Stoneware, painted
inv. no. 84-130

In shape and decoration, this extravagant coffee set calls to mind
the avantgarde style of the Bauhaus. The design came from potter
Margarete Heymann-Marks (1899–1990), who studied at the
Bauhaus. The set was made at the Haël workshop in Marwitz, near
Velten in Brandenburg, which Margarete Heymann and Dr Gustav
Loebenstein founded in 1923. The couple married shortly after, and
used the initials of their surnames as the name of their business.
After the death of her husband in 1927, Margarete Heymann ran the
business by herself—and with great success. The household ware,
with its abstract decoration inspired by the art of Kandinsky, was
sold as far afield as America.

The Nazi take-over of power in 1933 was a disaster for Margarete
Heymann. As a Jew, she was not only forced to sell her business but
had her products reviled as supposed examples of 'degenerate
functionalism'. She emigrated to Britain. The new proprietor of the
workshop in Marwitz was Hedwig Bollhagen. *CK*

Tea set

EMMY ROTH, Berlin, *c.* 1930
Silver, ivory
inv. no. 97-005

Emmy Roth (1885–1942) was another of the talented German artists of Jewish origin who fell victim to Nazism. Like ceramicists Margarete Heymann-Marks and Eva Stricker-Zeisel she was forced to emigrate in the 1930s, and founded a silversmith workshop in what was then Palestine. Her attempts to continue her creative work in a new environment failed and, prevented from doing her work by severe illness, she committed suicide in Tel Aviv in 1942.

This tea set created around 1930 with the slender, sober shapes and extended spouts is of a very high artistic and craft quality. Roth liked to combine silver with natural materials such as ivory. The set was made in the silversmith workshop she ran from 1916 to 1932 at no. 8 Clausewitzstrasse in Charlottenburg, Berlin. *CK*

Tea set

Rüppurr Fayencefabrik GmbH,
Rüppurr near Karlsruhe, *c.* 1925
Stoneware, glazed
inv. no. 88-232

A surprising feature of ceramic utensils of the 1920s is their radical
modernism. This tea set produced by the pottery at Rüppurr near
Karlsruhe also bears witness to a delight in experimenting with
shapes and colours. The unusual design integrates stereometric
basic shapes, futuristic-looking handles and a daring combination
of violet and gold. A version was also produced in yellow and silver.
The Rüppurr company was set up in 1923 by C. F. Otto Müller,
who had already been running an arts and crafts business in Karlsruhe since 1910. Its artistic director was the painter and potter
Heinrich Braun, who was possibly responsible for the design of
this tea set. *CK*

Centrepiece

TOMMY PARZINGER, 1928
Staatliche Porzellanmanufaktur, Berlin
Porcelain with overglaze painting
Height 20.5 cm; inv. no. 81-026

In 1919, following the fall of the monarchy, the Royal Porcelain
Factory in Berlin was renamed the State Porcelain Factory.
This gondola-shaped bowl is a good example of the precious
style of 'Prussian' Art Deco as produced in the Berlin factory.
Tommy Parzinger (1898–1982), one of the most creative
designers of porcelain at the factory, also became known as a
graphic artist and designer of wallpapers. In 1930 he emigrated
to New York.
The shape of this bowl plays with various design and decorative
elements. A circular base plate supports a fluted drum of a column,
out of which the bowl itself is formed. The appeal of the bowl
derives from the combined effects of blue and gold in the delicate,
semi-abstract leaves and foliage, which are capriciously held in
place by a gold bow. Tommy Parzinger's playful creations in porcelain were the most notable of the brief reign of Nicola Moufang,
head of the State Porcelain Factory from 1924 to 1928. *IB*

Art Deco and Functionalism 1920–1939

Vase (unique example)

ANDRIES DIRK COPIER, 1927
N. V. Glasfabriek, Leerdam
Amber-coloured glass with metal oxides
Height 21.1 cm; inv. no. 81-359

The vase was produced by applying metal oxides and blowing into a ribbed model. This caused the metal oxide layer to rupture, producing an interesting decoration. All phases of the work were done on the warm glass.

The Dutch firm of Leerdam had a tradition dating back to the 18th century, but in the 20th century it adopted a modernist design approach. One of those leading the way artistically was Andries Dirk Copier (1901–1991), who worked for Leerdam from 1923. That was also the date that the company began introducing art glass into its range—up to then, all its products had been utility goods. The art pieces were all one-offs signed *Leerdam Unica*, like this vase. The vase is a good example of Copier's clear, stereometric style in the period around 1930. *CK*

Tableware

LADISLAV SUTNAR, 1928
Loket Porcelain Factory (Elbogen), EPIAG
inv. no. 94-067; 95-036

In Czechoslovakia, modern functionalism in domestic ware was much influenced by the versatile designer Ladislav Sutnar (1897–1976). Sutnar established an international reputation as an architect, teacher, painter and graphic artist, but he was also well-known for his designs for the exhibition and sales organisation 'Krásná Jizba' (Beautiful Rooms).

Krásná Jizba had extensive contacts with the modern design institutions that mattered, for example the Bauhaus in Dessau. From 1924, Sutnar also worked with Artěl, a Prague studio for modern applied art with programmatic aims.

Sutnar won a gold medal for his work as the architect of the Czechoslovak pavilion at the world fair in Barcelona in 1929. The Czechs had been exceptionally successful at the exhibition of decorative arts in Paris in 1925, which indicates the up-to-date attitude that informed their designs. *IB*

Terrine with ladle

CHRISTIAN FJERDINGSTAD, L'Isle-Adam, *c.* 1940
Silver, horn
Height 18.3 cm; length of ladle 35 cm;
inv. no. 86-278

A characteristic of the silverwork of Christian Fjerdingstad (1891–1968) is the use of natural materials such as horn or amber for handles and knobs. The son of a lighthouse keeper on Bornholm, Fjerdingstad initially trained as a jeweller and goldsmith in Jutland and Copenhagen. In 1914 he emigrated to France, took part in the war as a Foreign Legionary, and after the war set up a workshop in L'Isle Adam. As a result of his successful participation in the autumn Salon in Paris the same year, he caught the attention of the old-established goldsmith company Christofle, which took him on in an artistic capacity.
This terrine produced in his own workshop around 1940 displays the organic and yet timeless style typical of Fjerdingstad. *CK*

Harp-playing Nix Vase

SIMON GATE (vase form),
VICKE LINDSTRAND (decoration), 1932
Orrefors Glasbruks AB, Orrefors
Colourless glass, matt-ground, attached black foot
Height 18.2 cm; inv. no. 81-445

This vase with a nix has a counterpart with a nixie. The scene with the music-making, fluid figure of the water-elf fits in brilliantly with the undulating motion of the glass shape that Simon Gate (1883–1945) devised. The beautifully cut motif was designed by Vicke Lindstrand (1904–1983), who worked for the Swedish glass firm Orrefors Glasbruks AB from 1928 on. It is a typical example of the new decorative manner that Orrefors adopted around 1930. The glassware is no longer covered with fussy engraved patterns but features strong, thick-walled shapes decorated with generously proportioned motifs.

At the international exhibition of arts and crafts in Paris in 1925, Orrefors won three 'Grand Prix'. The company achieved a worldwide reputation with its cut glass, whose heyday was between 1920 and 1930. Later, other techniques (e.g. 'Graal' and 'Ariel' glasses) became more prominent. *CK*

Art Deco and Functionalism 1920–1939

Lady with fan

PAUL SCHEURICH, 1929
Staatliche Porzellanmanufaktur, Meissen
Porcelain
Height 46.5 cm; inv. no. 81-405

A woman of the world, wearing an elegant party dress with a large
ostrich fan, turning towards the viewer with a graceful gesture—
this was the fashion figurine that Paul Scheurich envisaged.
Contemporary critics loved it: 'A masterpiece of elegant line and
sensitive psychology,' they said. The figure was exhibited along
with six other porcelain creations by Scheurich at the international
exhibition in Paris in 1937. The manufactory was awarded a
'Grand Prix', which was due almost entirely to Scheurich's work.
Paul Scheurich (1883–1945) was one of the great porcelain
designers of the 20th century. No-one understood with such
ingenuity and sympathy the spirit of the Rococo that is inseparable
from the heyday of European porcelain. Inventiveness in his choice
of often serene but lively subject matter, precise craftsmanship and
a sensitive understanding of the inner essence of porcelain are
what distinguished this latter-day Rococo designer. His figures were
always mentioned by art critics in the same breath as his great
forerunners of 18th-century porcelain such as Johann Joachim
Kaendler and Franz Anton Bustelli. *IB*

Art Deco and Functionalism 1920–1939

'Berlin
Secession'
Painters

Karl Hagemeister (1848–1933)
TEICH IN DER MARK
POND IN BRANDENBURG, *c.* 1902

Oil on canvas, 154.5 × 236.5 cm
inv. no. 80-068

Around 1900 Karl Hagemeister joined the Berlin Secession, even though he was no longer one of the younger generation and actually lived as a loner in the bare landscape of the Berlin hinterland. Yet no other painter discovered the colourful beauty, mystery and special light of this region and put it on canvas in such a modern and sensitive way. In his great paintings he proclaimed the artistic challenge set by nature itself. For him, the purpose of these almost monumental pictures was to do justice to the living cosmos and reproduce it adequately. Nature was not still life for him but greatness and organic reality: 'I painted woods, wild animals, water with water lilies and reeds, everything large, full of light and full of motion, just as nature itself moves,' as the artist himself is quoted as saying ('Erinnerungen an K.H.,' *Süddeutsche Monatshefte*, 1934) *IB*

Karl Hagemeister
SEEROSEN
WATER LILIES, 1902

Oil on canvas, 60 cm × 92.5 cm
inv. no. 73-170

In close-up, like a detail of a larger painting, the picture focuses
on one of Hagemeister's favourite motifs. Almost exclusively a
painter of landscapes, Hagemeister lived from 1884 in the
Havelland, the area of lakes and waterways near Berlin. He was
therefore very familiar with the natural phenomena of the area,
and combined the artistic interpretation of light and movement
into cosmic images of psychological moods. The paint is often
pastose in his scenes, repeating the organic principle of nature.
Water lilies still grow in wild profusion in the lakes and ponds of
the landscape where Hagemeister lived, and their beauty made
them a favourite motif for his art. It was a preference he shared
with many artists of his day—scarcely any other plant featured
so frequently in art. *IB*

'Berlin Secession' Painters

Karl Hagemeister

STILLLEBEN MIT INGWERTOPF, SILBERTASSE UND FRÜCHTEN
STILL LIFE WITH GINGER POT, SILVER CUP AND FRUIT, c. 1883

Oil on wood, 26.5 × 38 cm
inv. no. 86-067

Karl Hagemeister, who studied only briefly at the Weimar art
school, made the acquaintance of the Viennese artist Carl Schuch
on his study tours to southern Germany. The two contemporaries
remained friends for nearly a decade. Schuch had contacts to the
painters associated with Leibl and Trübner, whose modern views
Hagemeister benefited from. Under the influence of Schuch,
Hagemeister took up still life painting, a genre only found in his early
years. In the sensitive rendering of the white tones in the reflections
in the silver, the signs of Hagemeister's later gift for refined colour
values are already apparent. The support, although still dark,
manifests a certain lightening.

The friendship between Schuch and Hagemeister was finally broken
off in Paris in winter 1883/84. In 1910 Hagemeister published a
biography of Schuch as a posthumous memorial to his former friend,
who had died in 1903. *IB*

Karl Hagemeister
WELLEN IM STURM
WAVES IN A STORM, 1915

Oil on canvas, 125.5 × 168 cm
inv. no. 73-190

Hagemeister discovered the beauty of the Baltic, in particular the island of Rügen, through his teacher at the art school in Weimar, Friedrich Preller.
In his later work, from 1908 to 1916, the painter constantly made autumn trips to Lohme on Rügen, fascinated by the anarchic, untamed power of the sea. Without using figures or boats as staffage, he painted the rolling, moving sea, the spray with its surging crown of foam and the broad expanse of the sky as a fitting counterpart. Working on these seascapes was a challenge, pushing the artist to the limits both of his physical resilience and equally of his mental dedication to a great theme. *IB*

'Berlin Secession' Painters

Hans Baluschek (1870–1935)

HIER KÖNNEN FAMILIEN KAFFEE KOCHEN
FAMILIES CAN MAKE COFFEE HERE, 1895

Gouache on cardboard, 65.5 × 98 cm
inv. no. 73-005

Hans Baluschek belongs to a group of Berlin painters whose work
was strongly influenced by the trend for naturalism. He was a
founding member of the Berlin Secession in 1898. His scenes of
simple people, workers, children and women from the lower classes
were a novelty. His depictions of what was often depressing reality,
combined with an unusual view of things, made his pictures appear
to be a logical continuation of the style of Berlin milieu painters such
as Adolf Menzel, Heinrich Ziller and Käthe Kollwitz.
The scene shows a typical Berlin inn garden. Six women of various
ages apparently dressed in their Sunday best have made up a party
round an inn table to eat the food they have brought with them.
The young waiter, who is already going bald, is a conspicuous figure
behind them despite having his back to us. The picture is sharply
cropped left and right, a principle Baluschek obviously adopted
from the new medium of photography. The composition is framed
by two figures, who, like the table laid for coffee, are only partly
visible. The faces of the women vary from vivid likenesses to near-
caricature. *IB*

Hans Baluschek
BERLINER LANDSCHAFT (AM BAHNHOF)
BERLIN LANDSCAPE (AT THE STATION), 1900

Gouache on cardboard, 96 × 63 cm
inv. no. 73-011

The Berlin Secession was founded in 1898 as an amalgamation
of artists who were against the assumptions underlying academic
painting. Among the new pictorial themes were to be the things of
ordinary life—social reality. Despised as 'art of the gutter', it often
showed the downside, the less presentable aspects of life. In this
Berlin Landscape the topography cannot be precisely identified.
Baluschek composes his picture from various elements—housing
blocks of rented apartments, railway arches and the street. It has
been raining, a solitary female figure makes her way up the otherwise

empty street, perhaps
on her way to one of
the city centre
cemeteries, because
she holds a wreath of
red roses in her hand.
Baluschek developed
a special technique for
his scenes of social life.
He favoured gouache,
which enabled him to
define the subject
more emphatically and
sharply than would
have been possible in
oils. *IB*

'Berlin Secession' Painters

Hans Baluschek

TINGELTANGEL
JOINT, 1900

Gouache on cardboard, 111 × 68.5 cm
inv. no. 73-010

The intellectual fashion for naturalism that invaded both art
and literature around 1880 made a deep impression on Hans
Baluschek. As a large city, Berlin had its fair share of social
problems, which were reflected in art. Bohemian life was so
far removed from everyday respectability that it exercised a
fascination of its own and provided an arena for social drama.
Tingeltangel were downmarket pleasure haunts. In this one,
beneath a bust of the kaiser crowned with the national colours of
the German empire black, white and red, a demi-monde artiste
performs to a male public on a small stage. Baluschek developed
a modern style of
composition early
on. The foreground
edge crops the
figures dramatically,
bringing the scene
much closer, like a
snapshot. *IB*

Hans Baluschek

DIE KLEINE STATION
THE LITTLE STATION, 1912

Oil on canvas, 80 × 100 cm
inv. no. 73-015

Born the son of a railway engineer, Hans Baluschek was fascinated by the world of railways, stations, tracks and signals. Railways
are a recurrent theme in his work, showing his interest in the
world of technology and mass transport.
The small station called Molkau is an imaginary place. Deutsche
Reichsbahn's index of stations listed no such name.
The vivid depiction of the gloomy atmosphere of a country
station, the dullness of waiting for a train on a grey, wet day, is
turned into a personal statement. He repeated the mood of
his picture in a novella he wrote called *Im Käfig* (In the Cage),
which was published in 1919 in *Enthüllte Seelen* (Souls
Revealed). *IB*

Hans Baluschek
BERLINER RUMMELPLATZ
BERLIN FAIRGROUND, 1914

Oil on canvas, 150 × 170 cm
inv. no. 73-017

This scene of a fairground in Berlin is one of Baluschek's master-
pieces, shown at the first exhibition of the Free Secession in Berlin
in 1913/14. Crowd scenes were always a dominant feature of
Baluschek's work, but shortly before the outbreak of war they also
appear in the work of artists such as Ernst Ludwig Kirchner or Max
Beckmann. These artists' different takes on Berlin as a metropolis
were entirely their own. Baluschek favoured scenes in public
places—stations, factories, taverns—and street scenes or the urban
enclave of fairground stands. In this painting Baluschek combined
metropolitan flair with fairground bustle. The crowd is a cross-section
of all social classes—respectable middle class and a cocky street
urchin with a cigarette in his mouth. The picture crops the figures
sharply at the bottom and sides—only heads are visible, and the
dog strains on a leash held by a hand we cannot see. Shown
predominantly in rear view, everyone seems focused on the same
goal—the large, brightly lit pavilion in the middle of the picture
flanked by trumpeting figures, a magical centrepoint and mystical
place at the same time. *IB*

'Berlin Secession' Painters

Walter Leistikow (1865–1908)
DER HAFEN
THE PORT, *c.*1895

Oil on canvas, 76 × 112 cm; inv. no. 01-009
Acquired with funds from the Stiftung
Deutsche Klassenlotterie, Berlin

The painter Walter Leistikow was a progressive, modern artist
working in Berlin in the Wilhelminian period. His stylised scenes
of Grunewald with its lakes were quite unlike contemporary landscape paintings in the orthodox style, and particularly contrary to
the taste of Kaiser Wilhelm II, who liked to interfere in the politics
of art. It is no surprise therefore that this port scene did not gain
the approval of the kaiser, who fancied himself as a painter of
seascapes.
Leistikow opted for a view of boats in harbour, but the rendering
is far from naturalistic. The rigging is seen as a graphic element, and
the natural colour of the water is abandoned. The predominant
golden surface, against which the hulls of the ship stand out,
transpose the motif into a magic, unreal sphere. The harbour—
both a destination and a starting point—becomes a metaphor.
For all his regionalism, Leistikow was a cosmopolitan-minded artist.
The attraction that the north and the progressive art of the Danes,
Swedes and Finns held for him is evident in this painting. *IB*

Walter Leistikow
GRUNEWALDSEE ODER SCHLACHTENSEE
GRUNEWALDSEE OR SCHLACHTENSEE, *c.* 1900

Oil on canvas, 80.5 × 121 cm
inv. no. 73-787

Though Walter Leistikow had, as a painter, close ties with Berlin and the Berlin art scene, he had spent time in Paris in 1893 and renewed his enthusiasm for Japanese art there. His subsequent paintings reveal him as one of the most sensitive interpreters of the Brandenburg landscape. Regionalism was much in favour in art around the turn of the century, but Leistikow combined it with the modernism of Art Nouveau and *japonisme*. The two-dimensional abstract quality, asymmetry and art of omitting everything secondary indicate that he was an artist who preferred the characteristic impression to naturalistic accuracy, His melancholy, dreamt scenes of a rather bare landscape became mood pictures of an inner existential orientation. Leistikow was among the founding members of the Berlin Secession in 1898, which put Berlin in the vanguard of modern art in Germany. *IB*

Willy Jaeckel (1888–1944)
IM ROMANISCHEN CAFÉ
ROMANISCHES CAFÉ INTERIOR, 1912

Oil on canvas, 101 × 100 cm
inv. no. 73-272

In his early days a painter of ecstatic, visionary pictorial themes,
Willy Jaeckel turned here to a different genre—life in the metropolis.
This scene captures the pandemonium in a crowded corner of a
busy café—a range of different facial expressions reproduced with
an edgy expressiveness. The subject gave the painter an opportunity
to show the pulse of modern life, an expression of the inner tensions
in the years before the outbreak of World War I.
Jaeckel trained at Hans Poelzig's Arts and Crafts College in Breslau,
but from 1913 lived mainly in Berlin, joining the Secession in 1915.
IB

Willy Jaeckel
BILDNIS DER FRAU DES KÜNSTLERS
PORTRAIT OF THE ARTIST'S WIFE, 1923

Oil on canvas, 81 × 70 cm
inv. no. 80-085

Willy Jaeckel was one of the great German portrait painters of
the 1920s and 1930s. In his pictures he combined Expressionist
flair with verisimilitude and characterisation. The portrait of his
wife Charlotte (1894–1950) shows the subject at half-length in a
red, low-cut dress, sitting in a chair. The upholstery of the armchair
provides a protective embrace, the floral pattern of the fabric
furnishing a decorative contrast. The surroundings are otherwise
indeterminate—Jaeckel opts for a spiritual, cloudy blue in the
background. The subject looks out of the picture with challenging,
earnest mien.
The painting was done shortly before the couple separated for
good after nine years of marriage. Charlotte Jaeckel went on to train
as a singer in Vienna, in 1940 continuing to New York, where she
took up astrology, esotericism and spiritualism—frontier zones of
human knowledge that also interested Willy Jaeckel. *IB*

'Berlin Secession' Painters

Willy Jaeckel
EMANZIPIERTE FRAU
EMANCIPATED WOMAN, 1925

Oil on canvas, 110 × 150 cm
inv. no. 73-285

Nudes constitute a considerable part of Jaeckel's oeuvre. Along
with female portraits, it was time after time the female nude that he
chose to portray. The role of modern woman in a changing society
is particularly determined by her relationship with her body. In this
picture, the female nude is shown as a self-confident, almost
masculine-looking woman in a heroically exaggerated pose in
which there is a definite iconographic affinity with the reclining
statues of the Renaissance.

And yet it is unmistakably of its time—the short hairstyle was
considered the symbol of a new type of woman, while the book
she has put down is a token of her intellectual interests. The
muscular body suggests she is keen on sport.

The emancipated woman, rendered in monumental form and
with presence, is the protagonist of a new age, though the image
of strong femininity as depicted here seems to hover between an
ideal and a threat. *IB*

Willy Jaeckel
DER BLAUE GÖTZE II
BLUE IDOL II, 1926

Oil on canvas, 94 × 78 cm
inv. no. 73-289

Given the almost unemotional renderings typical of his portraits,
still lifes must have held a particular attraction for Jaeckel. A series
of flower arrangements in vases bears this out. In this picture,
the combination of a floral still life with an exotic female statue ,
there is an additional dimension. The painting, of which Jaeckel
did four versions, also reflects the fascination of his generation
for the exotic, non-European art of the peoples of Africa and
Oceania. In the expressiveness of shapes reduced to primeval
symbols, an artistic truth was perceived that was seen as lacking
in European art. In the unnatural colours of the objects, modern
art found models of a free design that led away from realistic,
naturalistic models. Colour became the vehicle of an inner,
individual existential orientation. *IB*

'Berlin Secession' Painters

Bröhan-Museum publications

Inventory titles

Karl-H. Bröhan (ed.)
Kunst der Jahrhundertwende und der 20er Jahre (Fin-de-siècle and 1920s – Berlin Secessionists)
Vol. I: Berliner Secessionisten—Hans Baluschek, Karl Hagemeister, Willy Jaeckel et al., Berlin 1973.

Karl-H. Bröhan (ed.)
Kunst der Jahrhundertwende und der 20er Jahre (Fin-de-siècle and 1920s – Art Nouveau, Werkbund, Art Deco crafts)
Vol. II/1: Kunsthandwerk—Jugendstil, Werkbund, Art Deco.
Glas, Holz, Keramik (glass, wood, ceramics), with the collaboration of D. Högermann, Berlin 1976. (out of print)

Karl-H. Bröhan (ed.)
Kunst der Jahrhundertwende und der 20er Jahre.
Vol. II/2: Kunsthandwerk—Jugendstil, Werkbund, Art Deco.
Metall, Porzellan (metal, porcelain), with the collaboration of D. Högermann, Berlin 1977. (out of print)

Karl-H-Bröhan (ed.)
Kunst der 20er und 30er Jahre (1920s and 1930s)
Vol. III: Gemälde, Skulpturen, Kunsthandwerk, Industrie-Design (paintings, sculptures, craftwork, industrial design), with the collaboration of D. Högermann, Berlin 1985.

Karl-H. Bröhan (ed.)
Metallkunst – Silber, Kupfer, Messing, Zinn – Vom Jugendstil zur Moderne (1889–1939)
Vol. IV (metal art – silver, copper, brass, pewter, Art Nouveau to Modernism), with the collaboration of D. Högermann and essays by R. Niggl, Berlin 1990. (out of print)

Karl-H. Bröhan (ed.)
Porzellan – Kunst und Design 1889 bis 1939
Vol. V/1: Art Nouveau Paris bis Königlich Kopenhagen (Parisian Art Nouveau porcelain to Royal Copenhagen), with essays by K.-H. Bröhan, D. Högermann,

R. Niggl and B. Fritz, Berlin 1993.
Vol. V/2: La Maison Moderne Paris bis Wien und Böhmen (porcelain—Maison Moderne Paris to Vienna and Bohemia), with essays by K.-H. Bröhan and D. Högermann, Berlin 1996.

Metallkunst der Moderne
Vol. VI , ed. by D. v. Kerssenbrock-Krosigk, with essays by C. Kanowski, on the basis of preliminary work by D. Högermann, Berlin, Leipzig 2001.
Modern Art of Metalwork (Engl. edition)

Exhibition catalogues

Jugendstil-Blüten. Florale Dekorationen im Kunsthandwerk des Jugendstils (Art Nouveau flowers. Floral decoration in Art Nouveau craftwork)
Ed. by I. Becker and R. Braig, Berlin 1985.
[Bröhan-Museum publication no.1]
(out of print)

Neuerwerbungen für das Bröhan-Museum Berlin (new acquisitions)
Ed. by D. Högermann and I. Becker, Berlin 1986.
[Bröhan-Museum publication no.2]

Berliner Porzellan vom Jugendstil zum Funktionalismus 1889–1939 (Berlin porcelain from Art Nouveau to Functionalism)
Ed. by I. Becker and D. Högermann, with essays by I. Becker, K.-H. Bröhan, J. Brückner, I. v. Treskow and P. Wex, Berlin 1987. [Bröhan-Museum publication no.3]
(out of print)

Ingeborg Becker Schmuckkunst im Jugendstil (Art Nouveau jewellery)
Berlin 1988. [Bröhan-Museum publication no.4] (out of print)

Metallkunst – Silber, Kupfer, Messing, Zinn – Vom Jugendstil zur Moderne (1889–1939) (Metalware – silver, copper, brass, pewter – from Art Nouveau to Modernism)

Ed. by Ingeborg Becker, Berlin 1990.
[Bröhan-Museum publication no. 5]
(out of print)

Ingeborg Becker
Wasserwelten–Das Motiv des Wassers
in der Kunst des Jugendstils (Water motif
in Art Nouveau)
Berlin 1995. [Bröhan-Museum
publication no. 6]

Ingeborg Becker
Zwischen Wien und Paris–Jugendstil,
Art Deco und Funktionalismus in
Böhmen (Vienna–Paris–Art Deco and
Functionalism in Bohemia)
Berlin 1996. [Bröhan-Museum
publication no. 7]

Ingeborg Becker
Japonismus–Ostasien in der Kunst des
Jugendstils (Japonisme–East Asia in Art
Nouveau)
Berlin 1997. [Bröhan-Museum
publication no. 8] (out of print)

'Das Licht kommt jetzt von Norden'–
Jugendstil in Finnland
('Now the Light Comes from the North'–
Art Nouveau in Finland)
Ingeborg Becker, with essays by M. Aav,
I. Becker, J. Gallen-Kallela-Sirén, M. Hausen,
P. Korvenmaa, S. Melchior, H. Saarinen,
S. Sinisalo, M. Supinen, M. Tamminen,
R. Wäre, Berlin 2002. (Engl. edition; the
catalogue is out of print in both languages)

Flämischer Glanz–Kunst vom Jugendstil
zum Modernismus–Gemälde und
Raumkunst von 1885 bis 1935 (Flemish
Art Nouveau to Modernism–paintings
and furnishings 1885–1935)
By Ingeborg Becker, with essays by
I. Becker, L. Daenens, M. Dubois,
N. Poulain, Berlin 2004.

'Schönheit für alle'–Jugendstil in
Schweden ('Beauty for Everyone'–
Swedish Art Nouveau)
By Ingeborg Becker, with essays by
I. Becker, G. Holmér, C. Lengefeld,
B. Nyström, E. Welander-Berggren,
bibliography and editing S. Melchior,
Berlin 2005.

Artist monographs

Margrit Bröhan
Maria Slavona 1865–1931 –
Eine deutsche Impressionistin
With an introduction by Wulf Schadendorf,
Berlin 1981. (out of print)

Margrit Bröhan
Franz Skarbina
Berlin 1995.

Margrit Bröhan
Karl Hagemeister (1848–1933) –
Gemälde – Pastelle – Zeichnungen
With an essay by Balthasar Otto,
Berlin 1998. (out of print)

Margrit Bröhan
Hans Baluschek (1870–1935) –
Maler-Zeichner-Illustrator
Berlin 2002 (2nd expanded edition).

Margrit Bröhan
Willy Jaeckel (1888–1944) –
Gemälde, Pastelle, Aquarelle
With essays by M. Bröhan, D. Klein-Elsässer,
U. Kvech-Hoppe, N. Ohlsen
(the exhibition was titled Mythos und
Mondäne–Bilder von Willy Jaeckel
(1888–1944), Berlin 2003.

Ingeborg Becker
Henry van de Velde in Berlin.
With an essay by Thomas Föhl, ed. by the
Bröhan-Museum and Museumspädagogi-
scher Dienst Berlin, Berlin 2004 (2nd
improved edition of 1993). [Gegenwart
museum series]

Museum guides

Bröhan-Museum Berlin
Ed. by R. Braig, K.-H. Bröhan, D. Högermann, Brunswick 1984.
[museum series]
Bröhan-Museum, Berlin (Engl. edition;
out of print)

Bröhan-Museum Berlin–25 Jahre.
Landesmuseum für Jugendstil, Art Deco
und Funktionalismus 1889–1939.
Kunsthandwerk und Industriedesign –
Bildergalerie
25th anniversary catalogue, ed. by I. Becker
and K.-H. Bröhan, Berlin 1998.
Berlin State Museum for Art Nouveau,
Art Deco and Functionalism (Engl. edition).
[Bröhan- Museum publication no. 9]
(out of print in both languages)

Bröhan-Museum Berlin–30 Jahre.
Landesmuseum für Jugendstil, Art Deco
und Funktionalismus 1889–1939.
Kunsthandwerk und Industriedesign –
Bildergalerie
30th anniversary catalogue, ed. by I. Becker
and K.-H. Bröhan, Berlin, Leipzig 2003
(expanded edition of Bröhan-Museum
publication no. 9)

Index of
artists and manufacturers

Index

Information

Bröhan-Museum

Berlin State Museum for
Art Nouveau, Art Deco and Functionalism
(1889–1939)
Schloßstraße 1a
14059 Berlin – Charlottenburg
(opposite Schloß Charlottenburg)

Tel.   +49(0)30-326 906 00

Fax   +49(0)30-326 906 26

info@broehan-museum.de
www.broehan-museum.de

Open
Tuesday to Sunday 10 am – 6 pm
and on public holidays
(closed on December 24 and 31)

Group visits and guided tours
Tel.   +49(0)30-326 906 00

Museum shop
www.broehan-museum.de

Friends of the museum
Freunde des Bröhan-Museums e.V.
Office: Schloßstraße 1a
14059 Berlin
(Thursday 2 – 6 pm)
Tel.   +49(0)30-326 906 28
Fax   +49(0)30-326 906 03
verein@broehan-museum.de

Ground floor
Permanent exhibition:
international Art Nouveau
and Art Deco

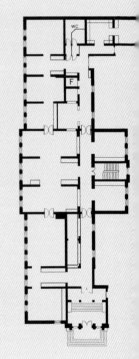

First floor

Permanent exhibition:
Berlin Secession painters /
special exhibitions

Third floor

Exhibitions from arts and
crafts collection/
special exhibitions

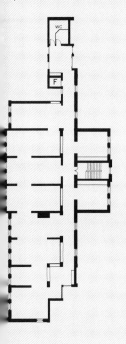

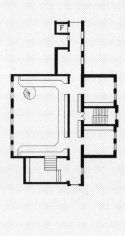

© Prestel Verlag,
Munich · Berlin · London · New York, 2006

© for works illustrated:
Bröhan-Museum Landesmuseum für Jugendstil,
Art Deco und Funktionalismus (1889–1939)

© for works illustrated with the artists, their or legal successors;
except: Peter Behrens, Edgar Brandt, Willy Jaeckel, Jean Lambert-Rucki,
Bruno Paul, Jean Puiforcat at VG Bild-Kunst, Bonn 2006

Prestel Verlag Königinstraße 9, 80539 München
Tel. +49(89) 38 17 09-0
Fax +49(89) 38 17 09-35
info@prestel.de
www.prestel.com

Prestel Publishing Ltd. 4, Bloomsbury Place, London WC1A 2QA
Tel. +44(20)7323-5004
Fax +44(20)7636-8004
www.prestel.com

Prestel Publishing 900 Broadway, Suite 603, New York, NY 10003
Tel. +1(212)995-2720
Fax +1(212)995-2733
www.prestel.com

Prestel books are available worldwide. Please contact your
nearest bookseller or one of the above addresses for information
concerning your local distributor.

Authors and editing Bröhan-Museum
Ingeborg Becker (*IB*)
Claudia Kanowski (*CK*)

Photos Martin Adam, Berlin; Angela Bröhan, Munich
Archiv Bröhan-Museum, Berlin
Cover: François-Raoul Larche, *Dancer Loïe Fuller,* 1901, bronze, gilt
Frontispiece: Karl Hagemeister, *Heron in Flight*
(On the Banks of the Havel), Oil on canvas, 180 × 110 cm, *c.* 1895
Back cover: external view of the building at
1a Schloßstrasse, Berlin-Charlottenburg,
Photo: Oltmann & Reuter, Berlin

The Deutsche Bibliothek lists this publication in the
Deutsche Nationalbibliografie; detailed bibliographical data can
be found online at http://dnb.ddb.de.

Translated from the German by Paul Aston, Oxford
Copy-edited by John Sykes, Cologne
Layout and production a.visus, Michael Hempel, Munich
Origination ReprolineMediateam, Munich
Printing and Binding by Passavia Druckservice GmbH, Passau
Printed in Germany on acid-free paper

ISBN 3-7913-3582-0 (English Edition)
ISBN 3-7913-3573-1 (German Edition)